10.95

For Mary Mihalyi
with very best wishes
Northfield 2.VII.86

REALITY AND RADIANCE

Emilia Fogelklou 1878-1972

Reality and Radiance

Selected Autobiographical Works of Emilia Fogelklou

Introduction and Translation
by Howard T. Lutz

Foreword by
Douglas V. Steere

Richmond, Indiana

Fogelklou, Emilia, 1878-1972.
Reality and radiance.

Translated from Swedish.
Bibliography: p.
Includes index.
1. Fogelklou, Emilia, 1878-1972. 2. Quakers — Sweden — Biography. I. Lutz, Howard T., 1921- . II. Title.
BX7795.F54A34213 1985 289.6'3 [B] 85-25299
ISBN 0-913408-89-1

101 Quaker Hill Drive, Richmond IN 47374

For Hannah Cecilia

Contents

Translator's Preface and Acknowledgments

The author of the memoirs contained in this volume did not entitle them "Reality and Radiance." She would have thought that a bit too presumptive. This title, however, is meant to reflect Emilia Fogelklou's intense search, as a young person, for meaning — for reality — in her life. The search culminated, in her early twenties, in an overwhelming inward experience that left her a radiant and sensitized "finder". Throughout her long life, what mattered most for her was the reality lying behind religious forms and "the radiance that came from that reality." In these words lie the essential elements of her life's story.

Gratitude must be expressed to Karin Westman Berg of Uppsala for permission to publish the translations of passages from the works of Emilia Fogelklou, for whom she acts as official literary executor. Similar gratitude is due to the publishing firm of Albert Bonniers in Stockholm for allowing this material to appear in English. Haverford College is to be thanked for granting me the T. Wistar Brown Fellowship in Quaker Studies for 1973-1974. This stipend enabled me to do the detailed research and writing that are the foundation for this book. Special thanks go to the staff of the Haverford College Library Quaker Collection: to Edwin B. Bronner, Barbara L. Curtis and Mary Hoxie Jones, all of whom helped and encouraged me in the work.

This book owes much to Emilia Fogelklou's friends in Sweden, who shared with me their papers and memories of "Ili" or gave practical assistance in a variety of ways: Ingeborg Borgström, Margareta von Braun, Gillis Hammar, Helga Henriksson, Gun Hilton-Brown, Margareta Indebetou, Brita Malm, Elsa Agda Marklund, Eivor and Sven Ryberg, Ingeborg Tegnér and Gunnel Vallquist. The staff of the Women's History Archive in Gothenburg, especially Asta Ekenvall and Beata Losman, were also most gracious in letting me work with the materials in the Emilia Fogelklou Collection there. More personal thanks should be given to my son, Jonathan Lutz, who typed the unabridged draft of *Reality and Radiance* and has taken keen interest in it at so many points, as has his mother, Eleanor Chalgren Lutz, whose assistance and support, often unnoticed, did so very much to bring this book into being.

Finally, it is to my college teacher, Douglas Steere, that the greatest debt of gratitude is owed, for it was he who long ago urged me to learn Swedish, who introduced me to Emilia Fogelklou, suggested my translating her writings, read most of the resulting manuscripts, and, at every step, has given advice, guidance, encouragement and inspiration.

Howard T. Lutz

Foreword

The Buddhists have a saying that "When the pupil is ready, the master appears." It has been my experience that when the situation is right, the "way opens." This is certainly true when a person like Emilia Fogelklou Norlind, whose life and works may have remained largely hidden to people of other countries than her own, is blessed with a gifted biographer who can unveil her life and message and share it with those who, in turn, have been readied to receive it. In *Reality and Radiance*, Howard Lutz has given us not only a moving sketch of the life of this remarkable Swedish Quaker woman of the spirit, but has gone further and provided us with what Francois de Sales would call a "spiritual nosegay" of her writings, which he has carefully chosen and admirably translated from the Swedish language.

Howard Lutz is a convinced Friend. He is a graduate of Haverford College and has a Ph.D. from the University of Minnesota. Early in his career, he taught for two years at Viggbyholm School in Sweden. He has a command of both the Swedish and Finnish languages and has been a frequent visitor among Friends in both Sweden and Finland. Howard Lutz is now a professor of history at the University of Wisconsin in Eau Claire and includes courses in Scandinavian history in his offerings to that university. He spent the year of 1973-74 at Haverford College as the T. Wistar Brown Research Fellow in preparing this volume for publication.

Emilia Fogelklou Norlind was for me one of the most spiritual women I have ever had the privilege of knowing. I first met her in Stockholm in the summer of 1937. She was then in her late fifties; a strong, vigorous woman with piercing eyes, a whimsical smile, and an endearing toss of her head when she spoke. The fledgling Swedish Quaker community of that day owed its existence very especially to Dagny Thorvall and Emilia Fogelklou Norlind who had come to know Friends in visits to Britain. Together they had sent in their letters of application for membership to be acted upon in London. Dagny Thorvall had died an early death, and among the superb Quaker women and men of that period like Greta Stendahl, Elin Wägner, Elsa Beijer and the Pestalozzi-like Per Sundberg, who had founded the Viggbyholm School, Emilia was heavily counted upon for her prophetic gifts and her wisdom as a counselor.

Emilia Fogelklou Norlind was a teacher and a writer, and among her many books she wrote what is generally regarded as the best biography of St. Birgitta of Sweden. Her counsel was much sought after in peace circles and among women's groups. The latter found in her a uniquely gifted champion of their cause, always rooting it in the humanizing and tendering powers she believed were women's gift to the community and in her view of the true comradeship that might exist between men and women.

She had suffered much. After a late marriage, the loss by death of her husband after so few years of life together had seasoned, but not quenched, the buoyant spirit of the woman whom I met in 1937.

In the summer of 1939, in a time when the world stood on the brink of chaos and catastrophe with the clouds of the second world war darkening by the day, we asked Emilia to come over from Sweden to the Pendle Hill Summer School to join a small teaching staff made up of Fritz Kunkel, a German psychotherapist; Peter Scott, a British community worker in South Wales; and myself, to lecture to us on her vision of the contemporary task of Quakerism. She came, she saw, and she conquered, and no one who attended her group that summer will ever forget her spirit. I recall her telling us once that she had had a serious operation a while before and that, in the course of it, her heart had stopped. The doctors had applied what was then a radically new type of adrenalin therapy and had brought her back to life. "Since my death," she told us, "things seem so very different!

Much that seemed terribly important before now seems not to matter, and other things that I had not previously even noticed now seem to me of great significance!"

In her Pendle Hill lectures, the Religious Society of Friends, which she had done so much to shape in Sweden, was depicted as a radical defeudalization of the Roman Catholic Church. Protestantism had hacked away at some of the Roman Catholic authoritarian superstructure, but much of this feudal structure of authority had all too swiftly reappeared in the clergy-laity relationships and in the worship patterns of the Protestant Church. She had found in classical Quakerism — with its corporate waiting on God in silence; with its liberty for all to share in the vocal ministry; with its complete elimination of a paid clergy; with its rejection of programmed meetings; and with its unique decision-making process in the meeting for business — a radical democratic Christian mutation that had dropped the authoritarian feudal structure and replaced it with a willingness to trust each ordinary man and woman with the inherent capacity to be a vehicle of the Holy Spirit.

There is an old Sufi proverb in which Allah says, "Give me your heart and I will give you my eyes." Emilia found that in the corporate practice of silent worship, she was asked for her heart, and that on yielding she found that she was given those Divine eyes that see all men and women differently, that see them in their radiance. When Tagore says, "For one who has known Him, no man is a stranger," he was referring to the new eyes that we are given, and it was with these eyes that Emilia looked out at others; and with these new eyes ordinary men and women lost their ordinariness and became the unique and wonderful people they were meant to be. It was no wonder that she was sought out by day and by night by persons who needed encouragement, and that under her eyes they came into a fresh sense of their own worth and to the meaning of their own callings. Here, too, was exposed the root of her peace witness and of her encouragement of men and women to experience true comradeship by drawing them nearer to this radiant Center that has no boundaries. Here, for her, was the only ultimate Source of authority in a radically defeudalized community that she, in middle life, had found in the Religious Society of Friends.

Augustine Baker, the seventeenth century Benedictine, had a

line, "Mind your call. That's all in all." Emilia Fogelklou Norlind would have kindled to this, for she was a Quaker for whom the inward Guide mattered. Early in 1948, I wrote to ask her to join with five other Friends in a small meeting that was to take place in Finland with the leaders of the Finnish Christian Settlement Movement and of the Finnish Work Camp Movement. We were to see if and how we could be led to perpetuate the memorable experience of true Christian community that we had known in working together during the three years of the Quaker Relief Project in Finland. She replied that publishers' deadlines and urgent work she was involved in would keep her from being able to accept. I wrote her at once that I more than understood and had hesitated even to ask her, knowing how pressed she was. A week later I had a letter from her saying that all of the obstacles to her acceptance still remained, but that it had come clearly to her that she must accept. In Finland, at this gathering, she helped us to arrive at a decision to establish Viittakivi, the Finnish International High School that has flourished in the years that have followed.

Only a few months before, I had sat in a Quaker meeting for business in Stockholm where a group of Swedish Friends had gathered in the hope of reaching a decision on whether to lay down or to carry out a concern of their beloved Per Sundberg, who had died suddenly two months before. Per had been in prostrate Germany several times in 1946 and 1947. He had seen at first-hand the mental and physical strain on the underfed and overburdened social, educational and spiritual German leaders on whom the reconstruction of Germany depended. He had proposed to the small Swedish Friends group a costly scheme of getting the necessary military exit permits, the Danish transit and Swedish entry permits, the Swedish food ration allowances and the rest that would be necessary to bring to Sweden some twenty of these German leaders as guests of the Swedish Quakers for a month of good physical and spiritual nourishment. He also had dreamed of getting an equal group of their peers from Scandinavia, France, Switzerland, Britain and the U.S.A. to meet with them for a week of their stay in order to let the Germans know how utterly they were accepted as comrades in the business of rebuilding the world in which they were all to share.

I knew that the rational judgments of the small group of Swedish Friends who had gathered was that, without Per Sundberg's leadership in carrying the central burden of what had to be done, they were quite unequal to the task of undertaking the concern. They had, actually, met with the regretful but full expectation of laying it down. The situation was placed before the dozen or so Friends present, and there seemed to be unity in the wisdom of a negative response. The group continued to sit in silence for some ten minutes before the clerk had to gather up the discussion in a written minute. Out of that silence Emilia Fogelklou Norlind rose and expressed her understanding of the feelings of inadequacy that had seized the group in undertaking this heavy task with such limited personal and financial resources. Then, like a prophet of old, she went on to say that there had come to her in the silence a wave of assurance that they must not fail Per's concern, that strength would be given them to carry it out, and that they must throw their trust on the ultimate Source of all true strength. One after another of this gathered company rose and expressed their uneasiness with the earlier appearance of unity in giving up the task that Per had left them. Within a few minutes three persons had offered their services to form a small secretariat to cover the principal tasks, and all had pledged themselves to assist as they could. Three months later the German guests were in Sweden, and their fellow social workers, educators, and religious leaders, both Catholic and Protestant, from the Western countries, were meeting together at Viggbyholm School for the memorable conference of which Per Sundberg had dreamed. Emilia Fogelklou's faithfulness to her Guide was the instrument that had made this possible.

In Japan they designate certain special buildings, sites, art objects, and pieces of writing as National Treasures. Emilia Fogelklou Norlind is certainly for us a Quaker Treasure, and I feel a deep debt of gratitude to Howard Lutz for giving us this precious window through which so many Friends and others can come to know her and be touched by her life and spirit.

Douglas V. Steere
Haverford College

REALITY AND RADIANCE

Selected Autobiographical Works
of Emilia Fogelklou

EMILIA FOGELKLOU

A Biographical Introduction

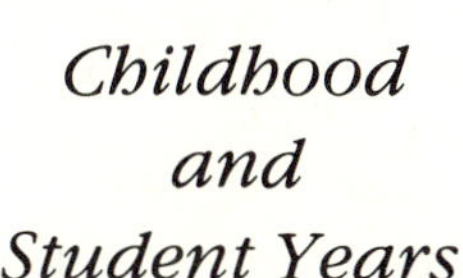

Childhood and Student Years

Emilia Fogelklou, the remarkable woman whose writings constitute the source of the selections contained in the present volume, was born on July 20, 1878, in Skåne, the southernmost province of Sweden. She was the fifth child and third daughter of Johan Fredrik and Maria Fogelklou. The family lived in the little seacoast town of Simrishamn, where the father served as town councilor and was much involved in administrative and financial affairs. J.F. Fogelklou's ancestors had been farmers, soldiers, and clergymen in the neighboring province of Småland, but he had taken a degree in public administration at Lund University and found his first employment as a clerk in the parish of Östra Hoby. There he met and married Maria Persson.

Though she was a farmer's daughter, Maria had received an unusually good education. Along with the housewifely arts, she had been taught foreign languages and other intellectual skills and had intended to become a telegrapher, one of the earliest professions to be opened to Swedish women. Maria's father, Per Nilsson, was an energetic man with a thirst for knowledge. He had been deeply affected in middle life by a revival movement which emphasized not only personal piety, but also a democratic and tolerant approach to the issues of the day. Maria Fogelklou had thus grown up in a home where the religious atmosphere was both pious and free.

Emilia's childhood was spent in a pleasant home called Backen on the outskirts of Simrishamn. From its windows one could look out over the farms along the coastal plain or over the roofs of the little town toward the Baltic Sea beyond. A large garden provided ample space for play and contained some tall trees in which a child could climb to a secluded perch to enjoy a book. Nearby, sharing the high ground, stood a great windmill whose sweeping sails inspired rich fantasies in the little girl's mind.

Simrishamn had, at that time, something less than two thousand inhabitants, most of whom were dependent upon fishing, commerce, or the local tannery. There were narrow winding streets, quaint little houses, and a close relationship to the surrounding agricultural area. Here, at her own request, Emilia began school when she was five. Here she played on the beach and saw the fishing boats return with their catch. Few childhoods, however, are free of sorrow, and when she was displaced in the family's attentions by the arrival of a younger sister, Emilia Fogelklou experienced a shock that sent reverberations far into adult life. In moments of rejection she found a refuge with her aged grandmother, a deeply pious woman whose blindness made her more accessible to the little girl. When the grandmother died, Emilia thought that "it was never as easy to be sure about God anywhere else *indoors* as it had been with Grandma." But out of doors it was different. There she learned to climb up on the garden gate to gaze at the sea or the sunset and to lose herself "in endless beholding."[1]

In 1890 the Fogelklou family left their idyllic home in Simrishamn and moved into the provincial capital of Kristianstad. Johan Fogelklou hoped that a district clerkship would improve his economic position and that the children could benefit from the higher quality of education available there.

Emilia had some difficulty adjusting to the new environment, but she soon responded to the intellectual stimulation of the better school. She was given to brooding and had to fight her way through several inner crises. When she reached the age of confirmation, she had serious doubts about undergoing the rite which would make her a full member of the Swedish Lutheran state church. Even in her early years, she felt uncomfortable expressing religious beliefs that did not have for her the ring of complete sincerity and genuineness. Eventually she resolved her misgivings, was confirmed, and would long remember the experience with warmth and gratitude.

In 1894, at the age of 16, Emilia Fogelklou had finished her regular schooling. Her love of books and ideas, along with a painful awkwardness in practical matters, made it apparent that she was destined for a career in schools and libraries. But she had to wait two years before she was old enough to apply for admission to the teachers' college. She spent the time working in her father's office and at home for her mother, who despaired of teaching her feminine graces or household arts. In the summer of 1896, she traveled to Stockholm to take the college entrance examinations, which, despite her fears, she passed with distinction. The National College for Women Teachers had been founded by men who had been inspired by the Swedish feminist Fredrika Bremer's belief in higher education for women. A decade earlier Selma Lagerlöf had studied there. Emilia Fogelklou spent three quite happy years in this institution, taking the rather strictly prescribed course for elementary teachers. Academically she did very well, particularly in mathematics and logic.

Her first teaching post was at a girls school in Landskrona in her home province. Once again she was following in the footsteps of Selma Lagerlöf, who had begun her teaching in the same school. Emilia taught there for two years and then accepted an invitation to join the faculty of a new school that was just being started along progressive lines in Gothenburg. In the spring of 1901 she spent a week at a planning session with the principal, other teachers, and some of the trustees. During the summer she enrolled in a special course, read John Dewey, and discovered the poetry of Walt Whitman.

The new institution was called Göteborgs Högre Samskola. It was a private coeducational school and began with thirty-one pupils and eight teachers. The principal or *rektor* of the *Samskola* was Dr. Artur Bendixson, a brilliant educator of Jewish descent. It was he who had most to do with creating the free and natural atmosphere that characterized the school in its first years. He welcomed his staff as the "world's youngest faculty" and inspired them with his vision of the school as a community.[2] The ideals he proclaimed have a familiar ring in modern ears, but in the Sweden of 1901 they were daringly new:

> We had been given a national cause to represent [wrote Emilia], and I suppose we thought ourselves very important, and, oh,

> so ready to make sacrifices! We taught during the day and prepared our supplementary texts in the evening. We made no distinction between work and free time. All of it was full of the same stimulating interest. And, of course, we were going to transform the world . . . .[3]

The *Samskola* departed from time-honored methods. Before tours were regarded as educational, the children were taken to visit factories and ships in the harbor. "The school was to be life and life a school," they said. Pupils and teachers were on intimate terms, and parents and trustees were welcome visitors, who came to contribute rather than to inspect. The young, mostly unmarried teachers, men and women, shared not only their school activities, but went on excursions, horseback riding and sailing together.

> We thought terribly little about what we were paid, although by the standards of the time it was probably on the higher side. Our school gave richly to us and we forgot ourselves, even our immaturity, in the attempt to serve it. And some of us were quickly consumed.[4]

Though Emilia clearly enjoyed this fellowship in work, she nonetheless felt burdened by being the only faculty member who taught religion. Since the rest of the staff seemed to be either not interested in the subject, or in reaction against it, she had no one to turn to for advice and help. Some of them thought she was too religious, and the *rektor* apparently considered her classes a sort of necessary evil required by law. In addition, she was put in charge of the morning devotions, which in this progressive school were known as "serious times."

> There lay a tremendous responsibility [she wrote] in being given so free a hand. She could make of the morning hour whatever her heart and her insight wished, yet she felt she had so little insight and so unprepared a heart.[5]

In several ways, the young teacher came in touch with a wider world. Along with some of her colleagues, she became involved in the labor movement and in socialism. More significant were the visits of outstanding intellectuals who took an interest in the *Samskola*. The book *The Century of the Child*, written by the controversial feminist Ellen Key, had exerted an important influence on the school's founders. Ellen Key came to Gothenburg to deliver a public lecture entitled "Men, Women and Children," and Emilia, filled with anticipation, was in the audience. "For me she was a legendary figure whom I adorned with unreasonable and childish expectations." Prepared to be overwhelmed, she found the lecture a keen disappointment. All that night she lay in a wild and tearful inner battle with the speaker. The next day she met Ellen Key in the school corridor. "She was so friendly, and though I tried to maintain a fierce air, it ended with her taking me in her embrace." Their friendship was to last a quarter of a century.[6]

The sleepless night of imaginary debate no doubt reflected Emilia's own personal crisis rather than any intellectual disagreement with Ellen Key. Despite the high morale of the faculty and her enthusiasm for the school enterprise, she was finding her classes in religion harder and harder to teach. She suffered a most painful inner uncertainty, the feeling that she was trying to teach something about which she herself was filled with doubt. Having no one in whom she could confide, she became increasingly depressed as the spring of 1902 wore on. In her deepening despair, she even considered doing away with herself. It was only the thought of her parents which held her back in the crucial moment. A feeling of brittle emptiness set in. It was in this state that she experienced "the central event of her whole life," a profoundly moving spiritual transformation. Her description of this experience is one of the most beautiful passages in all her writing. With this inward breakthrough came certainty of the Reality she had been seeking.

The immensity of this experience did not, however, blot out or destroy Emilia Fogelklou's intellectual conscience. Rather it gave impetus to a much more purposeful mental life, for she felt that she must come to a fuller comprehension of what it all implied. She began a second year of teaching at the *Samskola*, but apparently the work did not totally satisfy her, for one day toward spring in 1903, as she was walking in the street, she had a "definite inner bidding" to leave the school and prepare herself for the matriculation examinations that were required for full-fledged university studies. Through friends in Gothenburg, she obtained a tutoring post on an estate in Skåne, near enough to Lund to allow her to commute to lessons. Her duties were not onerous and her studies went smoothly, so that her sense of inner exultation was undisturbed. In a little pine grove she found a place to which she could withdraw for prayer. "There she brought everyone into her inner world, including those she did not understand." On clear nights she could slip out of her room on the ground floor of the manor house and wander out under the stars. Sometimes, during such nightly wanderings across the broad level stretches of the Skåne plain, there came the inspiration for short prose poems. These compositions, she tells us, "were not so much an effort at literary productions as keepsakes of the creative state of her soul."[7]

The year 1903 saw the beginning of her literary career in the sense that she was able to publish a volume of the short talks she had given at the *Samskola's* morning devotions. These forty sermonettes are most often based on Biblical themes, but among them are others dealing with St. Francis, Joan of Arc and Luther. They are free of the condescension so often found in older "edifying literature for children," and yet they are filled with warmth and spirit. The author was not yet twenty-five when she produced them.

Emilia Fogelklou also became known for her ideas about teaching religion in school. In November 1903, she was invited back to Gothenburg for several days to deliver two lectures which she entitled, "Concerning Religious Education." In them she asserted that while it was desirable for religion teachers to increase their store of Biblical and other religious information, they must nevertheless realize that religion in its true meaning can never be imparted, like scientific knowledge or language skills, through a course in school.

> She spoke out of what had come to her since the wellspring experience and had unfolded within her during the starry night on the plain. But the intensity and intimacy of the experience made for reticence in expressing it. She felt herself lucid and exalted, nearer to the world she came from than the one she was speaking to.[8]

She was indeed heartened by the response to her lectures and wrote that she came away "with joyful certainty that she had found *the great church* where there was a place for everyone." The next year she was able to get her two lectures published. Among those who reviewed them was a theology professor at Uppsala, Nathan Söderblom, who found in the lectures "some most moving passages."[9]

When Emilia had passed her matriculation examinations, she returned to the school in Gothenburg and taught another year before leaving to pursue advanced studies on the university level. There must have been much poignancy in leaving the outward site of her great inner discovery. Thirty years afterward, she alluded to this emotion in her address at a *Samskola* anniversary celebration:

> When someone has long been away from the mountain where he first saw the bush burning, there arises within him both longing and anxiety when the path and the place come to mind. Longing — for think, if the flame should be alive and shining still, as it is in memory. Anxiety — for think, if in its place there should be only bush and foliage![10]

After leaving Gothenburg, Emilia spent the summer in a little fishing village not far from her birthplace. She came there to write and read. Early in the summer, she produced an imaginative account of the prophet Hosea and his wife Gomer. Then she turned to a large volume in German, lent to her by a friend. It was Otto Weininger's *Sex and Character*, a six hundred page tome first published in 1903 and already in its fifth German edition when Emilia read it in 1905. A Viennese Jew who committed suicide shortly after gaining his doctorate at the age of 23, Weininger had exhaustively formulated his anti-feminist and anti-semitic views in this widely circulated book. He maintained that only the male is productive, intelligent and moral, whereas the female element is negative and incapable of genius. In his view, the woman was characterized by "organic mendacity," "incapacity for truth," and hysteria. "Woman has no part in the ontological reality," he declared. "Woman is directionless, neither good nor evil, neither angel nor devil . . . . Woman does not exist. *Die Frau also ist nicht.*[11]

As she progressed through the book, Emilia Fogelklou became more and more indignant, but her intellectual conscience drove her to read on to the very end. Here, indeed, was a painful and abrasive test of her sense of reality. It was all the more abrasive, since she had not yet acquired the psychological insight to perceive how sick a book it was. Here and there in it she found statements that contained strikingly valid points, which made her feel the work deserved to be taken seriously. For months she wrestled with Weininger day and night. Her own reality was not destroyed, but the book left some enduring marks on her personality.

In the first place, Weininger made Emilia Fogelklou more conscious than ever before of her status as a woman. She identified more clearly with all other women. She was prepared to admit that some of Weininger's criticism was justified, but she knew that she had experienced things which Weininger denied a woman could experience. This knowledge impelled her to try to eliminate from her life those feminine weaknesses and faults which he so cruelly castigated. He claimed that women could not endure solitude — she spent many summers quite alone in small huts in the mountains or by the sea. Weininger denounced women's "*Verschmolzenheit*" (flabbiness) — she cultivated being caustic and made a point of disagreeing. She consciously avoided borrowing others' ideas, since Weininger said women were incapable of originality. She also tried to avoid showing any feminine charm in smiles or gestures, things for which Weininger had expressed such contempt. For someone who from childhood had been given to open and enthusiastic expression of feelings, such a stiff and unfriendly bearing was by no means easy or natural. She later met other women who had wrestled with Weininger and saw that some of them had been permanently injured by the experience.

The first direct literary fruit of this encounter was a brief dialogue published in 1911 in the important collection of her early writings entitled *Medan gräset gror (While the Grass Grows*). In the dialogue a young woman, Signe, discusses Weininger's ideas with her brother. She takes up the notion of "*die Verschmolzenheit der Frau*" and acknowledges that it is "a real weakness, the reverse side of a strength — the feeling of being related to all life, part of a woman's make-up because she senses what life costs."[12] When the brother gets her to admit that women have not as often been politicians, poets, scientists, and the like, Signe explains:

> In the first place, women's task is not to give form to institutions or thoughts or images, but rather to create an atmosphere which gives to thoughts a richer meaning and bestows upon institutions a new value. — You will see that the time is coming when the matter of spiritual atmosphere will be treated as more than "mere air."[13]

Farther on Signe sounds a note that gives the volume its title and which caught the attention of many women of that generation:

> Isn't it true that, for your consciences, whatever positions you may occupy in life, the duty to ideas — that is, institutions, laws, the country, etc. — takes precedence over the duty to individuals? You have to see to it that "the grass grows" out there in the field. But our primary duty is to see to it that "no cow dies in the meantime." Because for us the duty to human beings is more important than the duty to an idea. And conversely, we think that crimes against persons are more heinous than crimes against principle.[14]

Finally the brother demands to know if Signe doesn't really wish she had been a boy.

> No! for I believe in a new person within both woman and man. A free, happy, healthy and richly endowed womanly person is what I believe in, someone who, whether or not she is married and has her own children to care for, is always sensitive to what is human, whereas you men prefer to look at things objectively. All the material objects and all the intellectual achievements to which she may feel committed are still only external matters in contrast to the deep certainty that the most extraordinary book is far less extraordinary than the simplest living soul.[15]

In the beginning of 1906, Emilia Fogelklou enrolled at the University of Uppsala. Here she came under the tutelage of one of Sweden's greatest religious figures, Nathan Söderblom. He was then a professor of theology and an internationally-known religious historian. In 1914 he would become the archbishop of Uppsala, primate of the Swedish Church. Emilia first took a liberal arts degree and then went on to study theology. The years at Uppsala (1906-1909) were very significant in the development of her scholarly qualities. She responded enthusiastically, though certainly not uncritically, to many of her teachers, and she also took a lively part in student activities, especially in the Student Christian Movement. Here she met several lifelong friends such as Dagny Thorvall, a warm-hearted and devoted young woman who, like Emilia Fogelklou, ultimately found her spiritual home in the Society of Friends. During these Uppsala years, she published a short biography of Saint Francis of Assisi, the work being an outgrowth of a seminar with Professor Söderblom. One of the first in Sweden to become an ardent admirer of Walt Whitman, she translated a number of his poems and lectured about him to various university groups. At a student summer conference in 1908, she delivered a series of talks on the Hebrew prophets, whose words had acquired intense meaning for her after the great breakthrough in Gothenburg. She continued to experience a rich inner life that found expression in her diary and letters to friends, as well as in poetry and imaginative tales. Her "Song for Pentecost" contains the lines:

> When some person's God's will
> has grown so strong
> that it alone lives,
> When someone has got rid of his devil,
> has doomed it to death and forgotten it,
> and cannot remember anything else but God,
> not the priest's,
> not his friend's,
> not the book's,
> but his very own God,
> When someone's whole soul
> in words and deeds and being is opened
> before this very own God,
> Then that person's Pentecost is upon him.[16]

Emilia Fogelklou's work in theology was completed in 1909. The formal awarding of degrees took place on September 15, when, as she modestly puts it, "for the first time there was among the candidates in theology one who was a woman."[17] She was to encounter much misunderstanding and even occasional resentment over this distinction. It was apparently difficult to see why anyone would take a degree in theology for other than professional purposes. When women priests were unthinkable to most people, there was little comprehension of the deeply personal reasons that motivated Emilia Fogelklou.

After finishing her work at the University, Emilia took a half-year appointment at the Teacher's College in Stockholm, substituting for her old philosophy instructor who had retired. She began looking for a more permanent position but had not found what she wanted, when there came a letter from Professor Söderblom announcing that the Olaus Petri Foundation, which he administered, was awarding her a traveling fellowship. This foundation had as its purpose to broaden the horizons of Swedish clergymen and students of theology by bringing distinguished foreign scholars to lecture at Uppsala and by giving grants of money to Swedes for religious studies in other lands. Hers was the first Olaus Petri fellowship to go to a woman and was to be used to study philosophical and religious movements in England, France and Italy.

Emilia landed at Hull on a Sunday early in August, 1910. The first month in England was spent with her sister Johanna and her husband, Alfred Wancke, at their home in Northumberland. Together they drove about the countryside visiting old churches and ruined abbeys, but also seeing something of contemporary church life in the region. She met High Anglicans and Irvingites, Salvationists, and Church Army people, and she was impressed by the readiness of ordinary individuals to witness for their faith. She attended a variety of religious services and recorded her impressions, such as those of a meeting of the Plymouth Brethren, the group to which her sister belonged:

> I accompanied my hosts one Sunday to the silent worship of the Brethren. A great deal of silence, no priests, the right to speak for all *men*, the breaking of bread, and prayer. When I first came into this quiet room with its crowd of people in deep silence, I thought of what I had heard about the Quakers. But I soon found great differences. Beside the rite of the communion meal, there were certain doctrinal points concerning the congregation and the atonement, a marked biblicism as well as an absolute observance of the rule, "Let your women keep silence in the churches." Yet I experienced true worship that Sunday.[18]

After this happy month with her relatives in the north of England, she traveled to London and began to make contact with the religious leaders to whom she had introductions from Professor Söderblom. The most meaningful of all of these was undoubtedly Baron Friedrich von Hügel, a Catholic Modernist layman. Von Hügel and Söderblom had become acquainted through reading each other's books and through correspondence. Despite recognized differences, each of these very ecumenical men held the other in high esteem. When Emilia Fogelklou met him in 1910, von Hügel was most disheartened over the devastation of the Modernist movement wrought by Pius X's decrees of condemnation. On September 1, the pope had required an anti-Modernist oath of all clergymen and of selected lay people.

> Von Hügel was then not sixty years of age. But his hair was grey, and his eyes heavy, and only with the greatest effort could he raise himself out of his armchair. He had to use a hearing trumpet to converse. Sorrow and fatigue enveloped his outward form. He seemed to me far older than he was.[19]

One weekend in October, just before leaving England for France, she visited a Reformed Jewish synagogue and a Quaker meeting. This was the first time that Emilia Fogelklou attended a meeting for worship after the manner of Friends, but her reactions seem not to have been especially noteworthy, for she says nothing about them in her autobiography. She met T. Edmund Harvey, a Friend who was the warden of Toynbee Hall and a member of Parliament. These first contacts with the Quakers were the result of von Hügel's introductions. As she left England, she received from him a note accompanying another letter of introduction:

> I hope that you will deeply, humbly and forgetful of self, grow in love to God and man and that you will conscientiously involve yourself in the conflict, distress and dust of this world, and return as well to be inwardly gathered.[20]

The weeks in Paris brought Emilia Fogelklou a series of most vivid experiences, not the least significant of which came from her frequent visits to the Louvre. Making use of letters of introduction from both Professor Söderblom and Baron von Hügel, she spent many hours calling upon Catholic Modernists, Biblical scholars, and philosophers. She went to see Protestant pastors and theologians as well as a number of more unconventional individuals and groups. While in Sweden she had become acquainted with the writings of Henri Bergson and now eagerly used the opportunity to attend some of his lectures.

Emilia returned from Paris to Sweden to spend the holidays with her parents. Late in the winter she went by train to Italy to continue her studies as an Olaus Petri fellow. Her first stop was Venice, where the people were celebrating the fiftieth anniversary of Italy's unification. Here she visited museums and famous buildings, but had no special contact with religious leaders. From Venice she went to Florence and thence to Bologna where she attended the quadrennial International Congress of Philosophy. Here she encountered some misunderstanding and criticism of her status as an unattached woman. In Siena she felt much more at home as she visited places associated with the life of Saint Catherine.

In mid-April Emilia Fogelklou was in Rome for Easter week. The city was in a state of excitement over the semi-centennial celebrations, which King Gustav V and Queen Viktoria of Sweden had seen fit to attend. Emilia was invited to a royal reception at the Swedish embassy.

> As I was being presented to the king, some well-meaning soul mentioned my degree in theology, and it seemed to me His Majesty turned away in displeasure. But Queen Viktoria made up for it with a long conversation. Something that amused me much was to see how people's faces turned to melted butter in the presence of royalty. (And indeed one never knows, of course, how one behaved oneself.)[21]

Among her most important experiences in Rome were her visits to Casa Brigida, the house where the Swedish Saint Birgitta died in 1373. Here a Swedish Catholic convert, Elisabeth Hesselblad, with a couple of postulants, was founding a new branch of the old Birgittine Order. Sister Elisabeth devoted much time to Emilia, telling of her odyssey to Catholicism and to St. Birgitta. Emilia says that she found the Catholic in Sister Elisabeth less interesting than the woman herself. Although contact with the Birgittines was to mean much to Emilia Fogelklou's inner life as well as to her scholarly career, the conversations with Sister Elisabeth brought out into clearer consciousness the contrast between the Roman Catholic position of that time and her own. A few years later she wrote:

> For was she not obliged to exclude from the spiritual fellowship me and everyone else who stood outside "the one true church," while I felt I was wholly free, without anxiety or temptation to convert, to listen to, to learn from, and to revere this ardent self-giving spirit who with every breath sent up prayers for the soul of Sweden and with every fiber of her being worked for "Mother Birgitta"? For me there was a world of faith unrestricted by the walls of churches, and in that sense I was the more catholic of the two of us. She would unconditionally have regarded every inner experience of breakthrough as illegitimate, spurious or at best incomplete, if it occurred outside that church where Christ daily reveals Himself in the sacrament. "*Sine ecclesia, nulla salus.*"[22]

One can suppose that for Emilia Fogelklou the greatest attraction of all in Italy would be Assisi with its memories of Saint Francis. Yet her arrival in the Umbrian town was marked by an unpleasant and inwardly humiliating episode which cast its shadow across her stay there and may have been instrumental in giving the visit an even deeper significance. One evening at the beginning of May, she stepped off the train in Assisi to find herself in a heavy downpour of rain. Although she had reserved a room in advance with a family, it proved impossible for her to make her way there, and she was forced to turn to one of the large hotels. There they told her they had no vacancy, but agreed, for an exorbitant price, to let her sleep in a large closet which housed the hotel's signaling apparatus. At no point during her travels had she been so rudely and inhospitably treated, and as she lay in the dark and cramped space, listening to the various bells, she became more and more incensed and indignant. Then it dawned upon her that this was exactly the sort of situation in which St. Francis had counseled the patient and good-natured exercise of "*la perfetta letizia*," perfect joy. In a deep sense of shame which lasted several days, she saw herself as simply not good enough to come to Assisi.

The next day she moved to pleasant quarters with the private family and began going about in the town, visiting places associated with the life of Saint Francis. Many of them were familiar to her from her reading and research. It may have been her persistent sense of shame, she says, "which helped me perceive, as never before, the suffering of the *poverello* (the little poor man) who here had lived and walked and spread joy in spite of everything."[23]

At the great Cathedral of San Francesco, Emilia had for her guide a Danish friar, a man who combined immense knowledge of Franciscan history and art with a disconcerting cynicism. She found him not at all sympathetic with her ideas about the invisible universal church — "ice church" he labeled it — nor particularly friendly to naive views of the saints, many of whom had "tormented themselves and other people a great deal," he said. Yet their relationship ended on a warm note when, on her final visit to the cathedral, he took from the altar St. Francis' letter to Brother Leo and let her hold it for a few moments in her hands.

A few days in Perugia, where she also sensed the presence of

St. Francis, brought her stay in Italy to a close. She returned to Sweden in the late spring of 1911, carrying rich impressions of places and people with her from the months abroad. The traveling fellowship marked the beginning of a very productive decade during which she established her reputation as a leading teacher, lecturer, and author in the field of religion.

Early Teaching Career

A few miles beyond the northern boundaries of Stockholm, a group of idealistic well-to-do citizens had founded, in the last decades of the nineteenth century, the pleasant suburb of Djursholm, hoping to combine the advantages of both urban and rural living within easy access of the sea. From 1895 onward, the leading personality in Djursholm was Natanael Beskow. Born the son of an army officer who had given up his career to become a clergyman, Natanael Beskow studied theology at Uppsala but on grounds of conscience felt constrained to refuse ordination in the state church. He turned for a time to a career as a painter, but soon found a happy combination of his callings when he was brought to Djursholm as the preacher in the independent congregation of Djursholm Chapel. The following year he married a fellow art student, Elsa Maartman, who was to become internationally renowned and beloved for her illustrated children's books. Natanael Beskow's long life was spent proclaiming a theologically liberal, socially radical and deeply personal gospel. His Sunday sermons at the Chapel in Djursholm drew not only his neighbors, but many from the city as well, especially young people in academic life. In 1897 he also assumed leadership of a private coeducational school, Djursholm's *Samskola*, of which he was *rektor* until 1909. Even after relinquishing the post, Beskow continued to share in the instruction and to exercise great influence upon the school's development. It was to this school that Emilia

Fogelklou came as a teacher the autumn after her return from studies in Italy.

She taught classes in religion, philosophy, literature, and composition in the higher grades and found it "sparkling fun." On her way to class one morning she encountered Ellen Key walking with Elsa Beskow. The impulsive feminist seized the pack of blue composition books from under Emilia's arm and began throwing them in all directions. "A person like you shouldn't have to go carrying blue books," she explained to the startled teacher. Soon the books were recovered and all had a good laugh over it. But, unfortunately, there was not time before class to allow Emilia to assure Ellen Key that she really did enjoy teaching composition.[24]

During her first year at Djursholm, Emilia Fogelklou was invited to deliver a lecture on Henri Bergson at the 1912 meeting of the Theological Society in Lund. Since the literature on Bergson in Swedish was as yet quite limited, she was helping to familiarize her countrymen with the French philosopher's thought. The lecture was well-received, and the Society elected her to membership. She decided, however, to decline this friendly offer because she "could not consider herself a theologian, but simply a human being for whose life struggle theological studies had been a necessity."[25] It was a difficult distinction to clarify to others, and it accentuated the uncomfortable position she found herself in as "the first woman" to earn a theological degree. It seemed to her that she was hemmed in by this notoriety, which cut her off from many normal cultural relationships and limited her audience. She was a hard person to classify, for she was not a literary figure in the usual sense, and she stood outside both the established church and the non-conformist "free" churches.

The years around the beginning of the First World War saw an acceleration of the movement for women's rights in the countries of northern Europe. Finnish women had obtained the national franchise in 1906, the first in any European country to do so. Norwegian women followed in 1913 and the Danes in 1915, but in Sweden the conservative resistance was more firmly entrenched, and the goal of equal suffrage was not achieved until after the war. There were, of course, other issues about which women were deeply concerned, such as the right to equal employment opportunities and compensation, the status of unwed mothers, and the controversial question of whether women might be ordained to the state church priesthood. Emilia Fogelklou followed these debates with interest and occasionally contributed articles to the Swedish feminist journal, *Hertha*.

In her work at the school, she was confronted with a situation that seemed to test her convictions. One day she was offered a slight increase in pay. In response she sent the board of the school a letter saying she was unable to accept it. She pointed out that a male teacher with her qualifications would normally be paid considerably more. To accept the lesser amount, she insisted would violate her belief in the principle of equality. "It would injure my happiness in working with the people of the future if I were to betray for personal gain a principle which will probably be accepted in the future, even if it is not recognized today."[26] She learned that the board was willing to raise her salary from two thousand to three thousand crowns a year, but refused to commit themselves to equality, especially since they had already agreed to pay 3,750 crowns to a male teacher with qualifications inferior to her own. She remained at the embarrassingly low figure of two thousand a year until a general change in the state school teachers' salary schedule brought a modest increase.

It is not surprising that, as the first woman to graduate in theology, she was often urged to enter the debate concerning women priests. Her position was not quite what was expected, for she did not at that point feel it was desirable to push for women's ordination. That women were as well-qualified as men to serve in this capacity she had no doubt, but she did question that they should consider it a pressing need to obtain official status. There were other areas of greater concern to women, as she saw it. Moreover, the history of religious experience indicated that where there was an inner motivation to exercise a priestly vocation, no ecclesiastical authority could really prevent or control it. "For it is rooted in a vital world where woman and man, Jew and Greek, are equally responsible and obligated, not only in the priestly vocation, but what is greater, in the human vocation."[27]

When the First World War broke out in the summer of 1914, Emilia was on a hiking tour in the Swedish mountains. At first the conflict seemed to her, as to many in Sweden, to be something unreal and far away, in eerie contrast to the outwardly untroubled surface of everyday life. But as the autumn wore on, a combination of difficult personal relationships, the thought of the terrible events on the continent, and possibly the weather, brought upon her a period of mild depression. Her usual joy in teaching seemed to disappear. When she arrived at her old home in Kristianstad for the Christmas holidays, she learned that her father was suffering from an incurable cancer and had been given only a few months to live.

As she relates in the opening pages of *Arnold*, the second part of her autobiography, it was just at this difficult moment that she became aware of the man who seven years later would become her husband. The story of Arnold Norlind's letter, accompanying his translation of the first canto of Dante's *Inferno*, and of their first meeting in Lund in early 1915 is included in the present selection.

Shortly after Easter, J.F. Fogelklou died, and his daughter left the school to go home for the funeral. She returned to Djursholm in a state of exhaustion and tried to go into seclusion to recover. It was just then that she was snatched, at it were, out of her private sorrow and her normal work routine and thrown into much closer contact with the terrible realities of war. Emilia was asked if she would represent the Swedish YWCA at the International Congress of Women to be held in Holland at the end of April. It proved to be a turning point in her thinking, for through this experience she came to understand, more clearly than ever before, the intimate relationship between the women's movement and the cause of peace.

Emilia Fogelklou traveled to the Hague by third class coach through a Germany at war. The women with whom she shared the compartment had faces that already showed the scars of suffering. They related frightful stories of what their menfolk had experienced at the front. In Osnabrück the delegates from Scandinavia were held under arrest for several hours because of a friendly, but indiscreet, word to a young soldier. Here was exposure to another world. When she arrived in Holland, she heard from her host the tales of German atrocities against the Belgians. Instead of sight-seeing in the Hague, she went to visit a camp where seven thousand Belgian refugees were being cared for.

The Congress was an inspiring event for those who took part in it. One need only page through the official *Report* to be gripped by the fervor of speakers like Rosika Schwimmer from Hungary, by the steady patience of Jane Addams, the president, and above all by the touching confidence that women, through appeals to reason and conscience, could make a difference. Emilia played only a small role in the Congress proceedings. Her name appears once as a participant in the discussion. She is also listed as a speaker at the large public meeting on the evening of April 30 along with twenty-two other women. The *Report* lists sixteen delegates from Sweden. With a number of them Emilia was to have continuing association. Of these the most important was perhaps the novelist and journalist Elin Wägner who, some twenty years later, would also join the Society of Friends.

Emilia returned to neutral Sweden with a new awareness of the vast scale of human problems and human suffering. She had planned to take a year's leave to pursue studies in the history of religion in Stockholm, but instead, she spent the year with her widowed mother in Skåne. She did, however, undertake a modest service in the cause of peace. She traveled about southern Sweden delivering a lecture on the practical aspects of international cooperation.

The most important visible fruits of this year at home were the articles and books she produced. For *Hertha* and for the YWCA magazine she wrote articles about the Hague Congress. The Hebrew prophets had long been a source of strength and inspiration, but in the anguish and passion of wartime, these "earliest spokesmen for peace" became forcefully contemporary. In the autumn of 1915 she published her foremost work on the prophets — *Förkunnare* (Proclaimers), subtitled "A book for laymen about the prophets of Israel." In lyric prose she describes the inner struggles of Amos, Hosea, Isaiah, Jeremiah, Ezekiel, and several of the anonymous and minor prophets. In her introduction she indicates why she found them so important:

> Within nations, unity — between nations, a great desolation. Such is the riddle and the wretchedness of the present time. Never before has the national interest so dominated the will and efforts of individuals. And yet hardly any nation is prepared to assume its share of the responsibility for the world crisis. Instead, every attempt is made to prove that someone else is to blame.
>
> Under such conditions some of the Old Testament prophets acquire a new relevance. They too lived in an age of worldwide upheaval. And from time to time they raised their voices to

> express a national sense of responsibility for history. They were not dreamers, but speakers of the truth and men of action who, amidst the struggles of great powers and the wily politics of little states, kept boldly and faithfully pointing out to nations and to individuals that there was one true way, the way of righteousness. This book is not for theologians and Biblical scholars. It simply seeks to call attention to some historical personalities whom our time needs to confront.[28]

The following year there appeared another volume by Emilia Fogelklou relating historical scholarship to the current world crisis. Two long, important articles which she had published earlier were reissued in book form under the title: "From Chieftain to the Man Crowned with Thorns." The first part is a presentation of the lays of Caedmon and several other early medieval poets with emphasis on their portrayal of the Christ figure as a mighty Germanic chieftain surrounded by his loyal warriors, the apostles. The second traces the development of this image through several stages, as the accent was shifted toward Christ, "the bearer of sufferings." The author describes this process with reference to the teachings of Saint Bernard of Clairvaux, Saint Francis, and Saint Birgitta of Sweden, not failing to recognize that in the growing understanding of the suffering Christ, the chieftain-Christ was not wholly eclipsed. All this is presented with a richness and refinement of language that lifts this little book above the level of ordinary history of ideas or dogma.

> We who have experienced 1914 and 1915 have much to ponder. In all ages we human beings have easily gone astray when on new paths, sometimes because of cowardice or because of pride, because of shyness or vanity, at times through our obsequiousness or our will to dominate. It is all the more important, therefore, to penetrate to the deeper levels within ourselves, that we may be made ready to confront the image of Christ — not the "contemporary" image, nor that of a bygone time, nor even that of "the future," but the real, the living and present Christ-image, which "makes all things new."[29]

Often the best time for literary work came during her vacations. In the decade after her travels abroad on the Olaus Petri Foundation grant, she spent her summers either by the sea or in the mountainous region of Dalarna. Particularly in the latter area she had occasion to come into close touch with the religious life of some remarkable peasant personalities. Frequently she was able to share her summer existence with close friends from the Uppsala years. And, at more or less regular intervals, there came Dante translations from Arnold Norlind, a welcome addition to her summer reading.

After her year at home with her mother, Emilia Fogelklou joined the teaching staff of a newly organized folk high school at the Birkagården settlement in Stockholm. Birkagården had been founded in 1912 by the efforts of Natanael Beskow and Ebba Pauli, a leading social worker. Both had been impressed by visits to settlement houses in England and sought to establish a similar institution in a workers' section of Stockholm known as Birkastaden. Among those who were involved from the beginning were Emilia's friends Dagny Thorvall and Märta André. A number of other young people who had been touched by Natanael Beskow's ministry at the chapel in Djursholm took part in the various activities that Birkagården provided for the workers of the district as well as for their wives and children. Rather naturally there arose an interest in having some form of school in connection with the settlement. The Workers Education League (ABF) joined with Birkagården in setting up a folk high school. This particularly Scandinavian form of school for young adults had originated in Denmark in the mid-nineteenth century, to a large degree inspired by the ideas of Bishop N.F.S. Grundtvig. Similar institutions had been set up in Sweden, but almost invariably in a rural setting with a close-knit resident faculty and student body. The adaptation of the folk high school idea to an urban environment came later, and Birkagården Folk High School was one of the first of this type. A leading personality in the early years of the school was Gillis Hammar, a student from Lund with a strong sense of social concern. In 1915 he began a special course for seasonal workers that came to be called the "painters' school," since that occupation was so heavily represented in his first group of students.

In the spring of 1916, Emilia was invited to come up to Stockholm for a few weeks to assist in the painters' school. She taught classes in the history of religion, in psychology, and in English. This brief experience at Birkagården had been most stimulating, and, therefore, she was delighted when invited to join the faculty as a permanent member the following autumn.

The two years at Birkagården were probably the happiest of

Emilia Fogelklou's whole teaching career. Her letters from this period reflect the color of life in working-class Stockholm, the conferences in which plans were made to improve worker education, the classes and study circles, the interesting individuals of all ages who found their way to the settlement, and the warm-hearted camaraderie of the staff. The clientele of the school was radically socialist at this time, but despite deeply held convictions and rigorous militancy, it was possible to conduct rational discussions in an atmosphere of freedom. Emilia's service at Birkagården coincided with the period of wartime economic stress when food was in short supply and effective rationing techniques had not yet been devised.

The mood of depression that had beset Emilia in 1915 seemed to be left behind as she moved into the program at Birkagården. That she worked very hard can scarcely be doubted. On top of regular classes at the folk high school, she lectured at the Workers' Institute. She led study circles for students whose interest had been aroused in her classes and who wanted to go further in the subject. At the same time, she was publishing a number of articles and the second volume of her textbook in early Swedish religious history, as well as a collection of medieval saints' legends. A large part of the basic research for her very significant study of Saint Birgitta was done in these years. She apparently thrived under this heavy burden of work. The excitement and stimulation of Birkagården, the creativity and essential harmony, were often in sharp contrast to the drab life of the surrounding workers quarter or the tense and bitter passions that surged in Swedish politics at the time.

It was, therefore, all the more a keen disappointment to her when early in 1918 the death of a close relative required Emilia to assume financial responsibility for the support of several dependents. There seemed no way for her but to leave Birkagården and seek a job that would provide the full remuneration which her formal qualifications might command. When, in the spring, the College for Elementary Teachers in Kalmar announced a vacancy for a *lektor* in religion, Emilia Fogelklou applied for, and was given, the position.

She was able to postpone entering upon her duties in Kalmar until October so that she might finish her book on Saint Birgitta. This work had originally been conceived as part of a series of textbooks in Swedish religious history that she had begun several years before. But she had abandoned the textbook project and decided to write a more concentrated scholarly biography instead.

St. Birgitta was not a particularly traditional saint. After being forced at an early age to marry a young man who, like herself belonged to the highest circle of Swedish nobility, she bore eight children and assumed the manifold duties involved in managing her husband's estates. At the same time, she imposed upon herself and her family the strictest adherence to the rules of medieval piety. When her husband died in 1344, a new life opened for Birgitta. She experienced numerous visions and boldly sought to live in obedience to the admonitions they conveyed. Upon divine command, she was led to found a new monastic order, one that was to contain both monks and nuns. About 1350, she left Sweden for Rome, where she sought papal approval for her monastic rule and worked to persuade the Avignon papacy to return to the Holy City. After a pilgrimage to Jerusalem, undertaken at the age of seventy, she died in Rome in 1373 and was canonized in 1391.

In her portrayal of Saint Birgitta, Emilia Fogelklou stresses her womanliness, as seen in her sense of being the spiritual bride of Christ and in her mothering of the souls of those who were placed in her care. The author makes great use of the colorful images of femininity and motherhood that were so expressive in Birgitta's work. There is an interesting transformation of this individualized caring in Birgitta's relationship to her family and friends into a general concern for the state of the Church and the papacy. It is this feature which gives the book its importance in the history of women. Its appeal was not limited to scholars and theologians. For a number of Emilia Fogelklou's contemporaries among Swedish women, *Birgitta* brought an experience of liberation.

The first months at the new post in Kalmar coincided with the severe influenza epidemic that struck in the autumn of 1918. Although she remained healthy, a number of her neighbors and friends succumbed to the disease. She taught twenty hours a week, almost wholly in courses in religion at various levels of the teacher training institution. In addition, she was responsible for conducting devotions four times a week at seven in the morning.

While this was perhaps a normal burden, Emilia felt impelled to work hard in order to assure "that there would be both learning and life"[30] in her lectures. But she grew more and more distressed about the risk of falling into "phonograph Christianity."[31] When the pressures of school and social life became too much for her, she found relief by taking the ferry from Kalmar across to the island of Öland, where she could hike under the open sky and lie in the heather, "getting healed, getting the dust off my soul."[32] She felt she could not have survived in Kalmar without these opportunities to spend her Sundays in this way. But that sort of need was not understood by the constituency of the college. It was expected that as *lektor* in religion she should set a good example by appearing in church each Sunday.

In some other respects she offended conservative small-town opinion. Although the Education Code prescribed that religion be taught from an historical viewpoint and not in order to inculcate belief, Emilia's approach to the subject came to be regarded as spiritually dangerous by some of the students. Moreover, in leaving Birkagården, she did not abandon her interest in worker education, and some months after she came to Kalmar she began teaching at the Workers' School. Here she met responsive students and another segment of the town's population. This only further discredited her in the eyes of certain supporters of the church.

During the autumn of her second year in Kalmar, Emilia began to suffer from an unusual fatigue and an unpleasant eye condition that made her acutely sensitive to light. Doctors prescribed various remedies, and most of her Christmas vacation was spent at a clinic receiving treatment. The scholarly work came to a halt, though she continued teaching her classes. This gave her more time to ponder the issues involved in religious instruction. The discouragement about her work, as well as the uneasiness over her health, brought on another period of depression. She asked herself why she should find it so hard to teach religion, whereas a number of sincere and intelligent male teachers whom she knew seemed to be quite free of her conscientious anxieties over maintaining intellectual honesty. It occurred to her that being a woman might be the explanation of her difficulty, and yet she hesitated to discuss that possibility openly for fear of jeopardizing the opportunities of other women.

The Years with Arnold

When she had finished the school term in the spring of 1920, Emilia Fogelklou arranged to go on leave the following year in order to get proper treatment for her eyes. But most of her year's leave Emilia Fogelklou spent at the bedside of two close relatives who were dying of cancer. During the autumn of 1920 she attended her 79-year-old mother, and then, at Christmas time, they learned that Emilia's widowed sister, Fej Liedholm, had undergone an unsuccessful operation and was not expected to survive more than a few weeks. The mother insisted that Emilia should leave her and go stay with Fej in Malmö. There the vigil lasted until the following September.

Since her eyes seemed to improve in the spring of 1921, Emilia Fogelklou resumed her research work, making use of the university library in nearby Lund. It was at this time, after more than six years of correspondence connected with his Dante translations, that she became acquainted with Arnold Norlind as a fellow human being. In her autobiographical volume called *Arnold,* she describes how their relationship grew and deepened during the last months of her sister's illness. When that illness reached its conclusion, Emilia planned to take her orphaned nephew to stay with relatives in England. Just before her departure she met Arnold in Lund, and their conversation left little doubt that for both of them the friendship had a special significance.

But the unhappy experiences at the college in Kalmar and the year of watching dear ones waste away with cancer had taken considerable toll of her emotional strength. In England she sought relief in new contacts and in scholarly work. She went to see Baron von Hügel, who seemed healthier and younger than eleven years before. She paid a visit to the Birgittine nuns at Syon Abbey in Devonshire and attended a Quaker conference in London.

Meanwhile, Arnold Norlind's appointment at the university had come to an end, and he wrote to her of his longing to find some new channel into which he could pour his energies and his learning. Just before Christmas he would travel to Italy to study ancient maps and pursue his interest in Dante. Although he did not mention it to Emilia for another half year, he had been informed in November that a throat irritation was actually a touch of tuberculosis. He believed that a time in the milder Italian climate would restore him to full health. Through correspondence they agreed that their paths should cross in Germany as Emilia returned home. They had two happy days together in Berlin and parted with the certitude that "no outward distances could seriously separate them any longer . . . . They had been taken in hand by the Sun."[33]

Arnold Norlind was then thirty-eight, five years younger than Emilia. Like her, he was born in Skåne, where his father was a clergyman serving a rural parish. Considerably younger than his siblings, he was often left to himself as a child and thus developed a close affinity to the world of natural things around the country parsonage. After preparatory studies at the Cathedral School in Lund, he went on to the university there in 1901 and finished his first degree two years later. He had continued to live in Lund, completing a doctorate in historical geography in 1912, teaching and writing, with occasional trips to the continent for research. He published several books, ranging from a scholarly study of the Rhine delta's development in medieval times to popular works on the First Crusade and Henry the Navigator. His interest in the Middle Ages was very great and, when combined with a love of literature, led him to begin his work of translating *The Divine Comedy*. When his brother Ernst, who was enjoying a growing reputation as an artist and writer, entertained Rilke at Borgeby in 1904, Arnold met the German poet and, like Emilia some months later in Gothenburg, was deeply impressed by him.

In Lund, Arnold moved in a circle of bright young people who were attracted to radical views. He became the focal point of a small and intimate group known as "infinity," who met to read and discuss poetry and other literature. Among these friends was Gillis Hammar who was to play so important a role at Birkagården.[34]

Arnold Norlind followed a singularly disciplined way of life. He was a vegetarian and abstainer from alcohol and tobacco, but enthusiastic for physical activities such as bicycling and hiking in the mountains. While doing research in Holland, he had met an able and warm-hearted Swedish woman to whom he became greatly attached. But an increasing uncertainty about their relationship had obliged him to terminate it in 1913. The break was a painful crisis for both of them and a major factor in making him turn to what he came to call the "Dante world." The responsibility he continued to feel for this woman inhibited his reaching out in other directions. It was, therefore, quite signficant to him to learn that she had married at just about the time when he and Emilia were discovering each other in the summer of 1921.

In correspondence during the following winter, they discussed the possibilities for their life together. Emilia was staying with friends in Jakobsberg outside Stockholm, working on various projects — a second edition of her life of Saint Francis and a guide to the *Book of Acts* for religion teachers in elementary schools. Arnold was disappointed that the time in Italy had not been as beneficial as hoped, but he wrote optimistically of his return to health. When Natanael Beskow offered him a teaching job at Birkagården and the directorship of a new second-year course at the folk high school, the way seemed clear. In Jakobsberg they purchased an attractive little cottage that would meet their needs. They planned that Arnold would commute the twenty kilometers into town, and Emilia would have relative quiet in the rural surroundings for her study and writing. During September they were busy moving into their new home — and trying to find room in it for their combined libraries. At the end of the month they were married in a simple ceremony in the local Lutheran church.

In *Arnold*, Emilia Fogelklou has movingly described her life with Arnold Norlind, as is apparent in the translated selections to follow. Here it is more appropriate to give a brief summary of the facts of their outward existence and some attention to their literary accomplishments. For most of the six-and-a-half years of their marriage, they lived in Jakobsberg, spending summers in the Swedish mountains of Jämtland or Dalarna. There was an acute crisis in Arnold's health in the winter of 1924-25, as well as several lesser ones, but the doctor's prognosis had been overly pessimistic. By 1928 they were encouraged to believe his condition was improved enough to allow them to move into Stockholm and lead a more active life within the orbit of Birkagården. In reality, however, the disease was entering its final stage. The few months in the city were his last, and on Sunday, February 17, 1929, Arnold died.

Despite his illness, Arnold Norlind produced in these years an impressive series of publications. In 1923 he was commissioned to write a history of the great geographical discoveries of the fifteenth and sixteenth centuries, and in the following year appeared his study of the medieval city of Rome. His verse translation of Dante's *Inferno* had been published the year before his marriage, and he continued to work on the second part of *The Divine Comedy* during his years with Emilia, although the *Purgatorio* came out only after his death. In 1925 he published a brief biographical interpretation of Dante. The struggle for health in his last years forms the background for a book of meditations, *From My Veranda*, that appeared in 1928. It was to become the most enduring of his writings, along with a posthumous collection of essays on his favorite poets (Whitman among them) and a volume of excerpts from his early diaries.

Emilia, too, pursued in these difficult years an active intellectual and literary life. She lectured in Stockholm and on tours through the country. She spoke at conferences and produced articles. A number of lectures and articles were gathered and published in book form. The titles of these collections — *Leisure and Labor, Man and His Work, Community Types and Citizen Ideals, School Life and the Spiritual Life, The Psychology of Cooperation* — give some indication of the range of her interests in this period. In addition, she wrote guides for religion teachers and put together a handsome folio volume entitled *The Liberator,* in which the story of Jesus is told through selections from the Bible, the Swedish hymnal, and a variety of poets, and illustrated with color reproductions of Fra Angelico's paintings. For a popular devotional series, she compiled a book of selections from the *Revelations* of Saint Birgitta.

During the last year with Arnold, Emilia Fogelklou was busy writing one of her most significant works, a study of the early Quaker leader, James Nayler. It appeared in Sweden in the spring of 1929, and a translation by Lajla Yapp came out in England two years later.[36] While Emilia Fogelklou sought to make an original contribution to the study of the first generation of the Quaker movement in the seventeenth century, her book on Nayler had its greatest impact in opening up for Swedes a chapter of religious history that had hitherto been accessible only in a foreign tongue. What little Quaker literature was to be found in Sweden fifty years ago was either in English or in a few translations of books originally written in English. Emilia's work was addressed to Swedish readers and took their frame of reference into consideration. She produced an eminently readable, at points deeply moving, account that not only dealt with the striking figure of James Nayler, but provided a general orientation to the English religious situation of the 1640's and 1650's out of which Quakerism was born.

But Emilia Fogelklou's book touched a sensitive point for Quaker historians when it devoted many pages to the relationship of Nayler to George Fox. In the unhappy conflict that arose between the two men, she showed greater sympathy for Nayler and was quite critical of Fox's handling of him. At one point, she went so far as to compare Fox to Cromwell in his transition "from a democratic to an imperialistic type."[37] These words, as well as a number of others, greatly distressed Neave Brayshaw, the English biographer of Fox, and he appealed to Rufus Jones to write an article correcting the false impression that the book created. The London *Friend* had already carried a review, a rather favorable one, by Gerald Hibbert,[38] but two months later it published another by Rufus Jones who pointed out the injustices he felt Emilia had done to George Fox.[39] Non-Quaker reviewers in Britain and Sweden, knowing perhaps less of Quaker history, were generally much impressed by the book and commented on its excellent dramatic qualities and its skillful depiction of spiritual conditions. Even the editor of the *Journal of the Friends Historical Society*, in a brief notice of the book, said, "We venture to state that no Quaker biography of modern times has been presented to the British public in such literary form as this volume."[40] While that assessment may today be considered unduly laudatory, *Kväkaren James Nayler* is still the most vivid account of the beginnings of Quakerism to be found in Swedish and the only one of Emilia Fogelklou's books that has yet been translated into English.

Emilia was fifty when Arnold died, and, now freed of the practical burdens that beset her while he lived, she was once more confronted with the need to find some work into which she could pour all of herself. For a year or so, she taught at Birkagården again. In 1930 the Swedish-American Foundation awarded her the generous Zorn Fellowship to study sociology in New York, Chicago, and elsewhere in the United States. The poverty and unemployment brought on by the Great Depression made themselves very apparent to her during this first visit to America. She continued her writing and lecturing, but the permanent job she hoped for never seemed to come.

Life As A Friend

For some time Emilia Fogelklou had been moving toward the Society of Friends. Even in the days when she was studying theology at Uppsala, she had felt ill at ease with the state church. She was close to Archbishop Söderblom and to a number of the other leaders who were bringing a new vitality into Swedish Lutheranism, emphasizing its cultural and social responsibilities. But it did not seem to fit her ideals and needs. She was very open to the sort of Catholicism represented by von Hügel and other Catholic Modernists, and she found much that appealed to her in medieval religious life. But she was too free a spirit to accept the authoritarianism that characterized the Church of Rome. Her strong consciousness as a woman made her react negatively to all patriarchal forms of religion, and her commitment to a spiritually-based democratic ideal caused her to reject any ecclesiastical organization that had not freed itself of what she called "feudal" elements. She had had a number of contacts with Quakerism, especially since the end of the First World War and came more and more to feel identified with it.

When Emilia and Arnold moved into Stockholm in the autumn of 1928, they joined the small group that was then meeting for silent worship in the library at Birkagården, where most of them worked. In 1931 Mab Maynard, an English Friend whom Emilia had come to know when she was working on the Nayler materials, visited Sweden and apparently talked with some of the group about joining Friends. A few months later both Dagny Thorvall and Emilia Fogelklou sent applications for membership to the Friends Service Council, which had responsibility for the Register of Foreign Members of London Yearly Meeting. On November 5, 1931, their applications came before an FSC meeting, which Mab Maynard described in a letter to Emilia:

> For me the high light . . . was the half hour yesterday afternoon devoted to "Applications for Membership from Abroad." The "Foreign Membership Committee" had already considered these . . . applications and Carl Heath presented them to the Council (about 120 persons, I should think). In order of receipt he read Dagny's application and the letters which Robert Davis and I wrote in support. One or two expressed their happiness and *all* warmly concurred in welcoming this dear friend. Then Carl read your letter and those which Marion Fox and I had written in support . . . and I may not tell you the warm words that were spoken about you!! Then John William Graham with real emotion expressed the deep thankfulness of us all that two such fine and true servants of God were joining themselves to our fellowship.[41]

Emilia became almost immediately a quite active Friend. At the International Quaker Conference in Amsterdam in November, 1932, she delivered a paper on "Luther and Fox." In 1933-34 she came as a fellow to Woodbrooke, a Quaker adult college at Birmingham, where she did the research that resulted in her book on William Penn. During the year in England, she formed deep friendships with several Quaker women, as well as with members of the Woodbrooke staff and student body. She traveled to various meetings in England, to the Yearly Meeting in Dublin, and to the International Quaker Conference in Geneva. She also paid a second visit to Syon Abbey and the Birgittine nuns.

Upon her return to Sweden in the summer of 1934, Emilia committed herself to an ambitious schedule of lectures and study circles. But ever since the death of Arnold five years before, she had often been on the edge of sickness. She now contracted a severe case of pneumonia, which, along with other complications, caused a prolonged period of illness. At one point, she was not expected to recover and was joyful at the thought of "getting out of school away from problems and walls of separation." But, "death, just then so infinitely welcome, turned and went away."

As she was convalescing, her friends gathered a sum of money which they donated to the University of Stockholm, on the understanding that she would be employed to give a series of lectures over the next three years.

During the decade following Arnold Norlind's death in 1929, Emilia Fogelklou published several important books. Her volume on William Penn (1935), while not translated into English, has appeared in two German editions (1948, 1963). From an inchoate bulk of manuscript material, she selected and edited passages to form *The Autobiography of Siri Zöller* (1931), a unique Swedish intellectual who died in 1896. Using a combination of psychological and sociological approaches, she published a revealing study of the religious opinions of Swedish young people active in various popular movements. The best of her articles and lectures appeared in two collections, *The Most Ordinary Person* (1931) and *Protestant and Catholic* (1937). By the end of the 'thirties, Emilia Fogelklou had won wide recognition in Sweden as a *kulturpersonlighet* and had been the subject of interpretive articles by leading scholars writing for the best journals. As one of these concluded, "Her career is definitely pointing upward."[42]

If Emilia Fogelklou harbored any aspirations that could be called "upward" in a this-worldly sense, they were about to suffer a severe set-back. In the late summer of 1938, she returned to Sweden after attending the German Yearly Meeting of Friends held at Bad Pyrmont under Nazi police surveillance. She found waiting for her a letter from an academic friend who urged her to apply for a vacant Uppsala professorship in the history and psychology of religion. Very uncertain about her chances, she consulted three friends upon whose judgment she felt she could rely. All agreed she should try for the position. In order to strengthen her qualifications, she concentrated for several months on producing a scholarly study of certain aspects of the medieval Swedish provincial law codes. In November, she submitted her application to Uppsala with all the necessary documentation. It has been seriously alleged that there then occurred a number of maneuvers behind the scenes, by which the scope of the professorship was redefined in such a way that Emilia Fogelklou would be eliminated from the competition. In 1940 the position was given to a young man of much more modest scholarly accomplishments, while she was publicly declared to be incompetent to hold such a professorship. The full story behind this unhappy affair is yet to be told, and till then one must reserve judgment about it. In any case, it created difficulties for Emilia, as her income from lecturing fell off sharply for a time after she was declared incompetent. Although she struggled to overcome her feelings of bitterness, this rejection long continued to cause her inner suffering, perhaps because its pain was akin to that she had known in early childhood.

In 1939 Emilia came a second time to the United States in order to teach at Pendle Hill, the Quaker study center in Wallingford, Pennsylvania. Professor Douglas Steere had invited her to join the staff of the summer school that he was directing that year. She gave a series of lectures on "Individualism and Community Life in Quakerism," presenting a rather sociological approach to the seventeenth-century Friends. In the Philadelphia area, she visited Quaker meetings and schools and made some contact with the Black community, which interested her very much. At the conclusion of the summer school, she joined the directors of Pendle Hill, Howard and Anna Brinton, on an extended automobile tour to visit student work camps sponsored by the American Friends Service Committee. In western Pennsylvania, Tennessee, and Michigan, she saw young men and women engaged in volunteer labor projects for the benefit of people who had fallen victims of the depression. This form of social service motivated by practical idealism made a lasting impression upon her.

The Second World War began just as Emilia returned to Sweden from her months in America. As the citizen of a neutral state, she was asked to serve for a time in the Quaker office in Berlin. Since the previous December, when Rufus Jones and two other Philadelphia Friends had gone to Germany to intercede for German Jews, the office on Prinz Louis Ferdinandstrasse was attempting to provide assistance to persons who sought to emigrate. Until late November, Emilia was part of the Quaker staff and had many opportunities to observe the hardships of the Jews, as well as other aspects of German life at this stage of the war. When the crisis involving Finland's relationship to the Soviet Union became acute, it was feared that Sweden might become a belligerent, too, so Emilia decided to return home.

Although she had been rejected for the professorship, the faculty at Uppsala conferred upon her an honorary doctorate in theology in 1941. But such personal concerns fell to the side, as she found herself drawn into groups of Swedish young people who were seeking ways of lightening the burdens of suffering brought on by the war. She was close to the young academicians who started SISU, a student organization that engaged university youth to work for refugees and in planning for post-war reconstruction. Emilia spoke at SISU conferences and helped publish their magazine. She was even more intimately involved with another group of young people, known as "IAL" (for International Labor Teams), which was the brainchild of Wolfgang Sonntag, himself a German refugee. At meetings of IAL, Emilia lectured on her experience in American work camps in 1939. When large numbers of Danish refugees began arriving in 1943, IAL members were used in the operation of facilities for housing them. Some of the IAL young people gathered in camps where they could combine part-time farm work with training in languages and other skills they might need in war-devastated areas. Emilia was a tireless visitor to these projects, spending a week or more at a time with the young people, lecturing in the evenings on such subjects as the Quaker experience with relief operations. One of the participants in such a camp has since described her impressions of Emilia Fogelklou:

> From the beginning she gave this youthful enterprise a supporting hand. The direction was Emilia's — toward a human environment without boundaries . . . . She gave us unstintingly of her time and energy. What a flood of psychological and sociological learning she shared with us! What buoyancy of body and mind, what irrepressible contagion — as when at 66 she got lost with us in the dark woods as we were returning from the village after an evening session on biodynamics.[43]

In addition to encouraging others, Emilia participated directly in post-war reconstruction planning and work. Even before hostilities had ceased in Europe, she flew to England in December, 1944, to confer with Friends there on how the needs were to be met. The next year found her working with three hundred Polish women who had been brought from concentration camps in Germany for physical and spiritual rehabilitation in a camp in Sweden. Later she served for a time in the barrack that IAL had set up in Hamburg in an effort to do something for the people of that devastated city.

The unhappy attempt to obtain a professorship at Uppsala, despite its pain to Emilia Fogelklou and loss to the academic world, did provide an incentive to put into publishable form her research on the traces of matriarchal society found in Swedish medieval sources. In 1941 there appeared a slender volume containing nine articles with the title *Beyond Birgitta*. Here Emilia presented her case for believing that the original provincial law-codes contained evidence of a prehistoric equality of the sexes and perhaps even of a primitive Germanic matriarchy. This view was at variance with the generally accepted interpretation of contemporary scholars, but it received serious consideration in several quarters. In the same book, Emilia took up certain motifs occurring in Saint Birgitta's *Revelations* to show that the treatment of matters such as marriage, childbirth, household arts, and witchcraft also contained vestiges of a time when the position of women was more favorable than it became under the influence of the church and feudalism.

These ideas about the earlier status of women were of particular interest to Emilia's friend and fellow Quaker, Elin Wägner. A feminist novelist, she was working to express the anguish and urgency she felt as she watched the progress of the Second World War. The two women had known each other since they were participants in the Hague Congress of 1915, and their paths had crossed many times in their common concern for peace and the women's movement. It was Emilia who led Elin Wägner into the writings of Bachofen, Briffault, and others who dealt with the early history of the family. This study constituted an important element in Elin Wägner's non-fiction work entitled *The Alarm Clock* (1942), a deeply felt appeal to women in all lands to resist the destructive forces not only of war, but of dehumanizing industrialism and the ruthless exploitation of the natural environment.[44]

When Emilia Fogelklou reached the age of 68, she thought that the time had come for her to withdraw from the world into a quiet life. She chose a little cottage in the country several hours by train from Stockholm. But even here she was in demand. She was asked to give two days a week to psychological counseling in a nearby factory town. Various groups invited her to speak at meetings and conferences, and there came new opportunities to serve the Society of Friends. In 1947 she was elected president of the Friends Historical Society of London. In 1949 she represented Friends as an observer at a World Council of Churches meeting in Chichester. There were yearly meetings and other Quaker gatherings in Norway and Finland as well as Sweden.

Since her student days, Emilia had hoped to visit the eastern Mediterranean lands that had given birth to western culture. Now in her early seventies, like St. Birgitta at a similar age, she was able to make a pilgrimage to the Holy Land. In March, 1951, she spent several weeks in Israel, where she saw scenes of almost Biblical antiquity, as well as the bustling energy of the new Jewish state in its early struggles. The tragic conflict with the Arabs deeply perplexed her, and she sought eagerly for signs of a spirit of reconciliation at work there. She paid visits to individual homes, schools, kibbutzim, and other institutions, where she was received with warm hospitality. The youthful enthusiasm and practical devotion of the new colonists evoked her admiration. She was also able to have serious conversations with several of Israel's spiritual leaders, such as the philosopher Hugo Bergman and the Nobel Prize winning writer S.J.Agnon. Leaving Israel, Emilia traveled to Greece, there to realize an old dream she had once shared with Arnold — to visit sites associated with classical Greek antiquity. During the days she spent at Delphi, she had a particularly happy sense of his presence with her as she climbed about the ruins of the ancient temple.

Emilia Fogelklou's most significant literary work in these years arose out of very personal experiences, rather than as a reflection of the vast actions on the world scene. In 1944, fifteen years after her husband's death, she published *Arnold*. While it is chiefly a biography of Arnold Norlind, she wrote about him from her own point of view, and thus much of the work is autobiographical as well. After a chapter describing her first contacts with Arnold, the deepening friendship between them, and their days together in Berlin in December, 1921, she devoted three long chapters to an account of his earlier life up to that point. For this section she drew heavily upon Arnold's letters and diaries and supplemented these with the recollections of his sister and other relatives and friends. The final six chapters, covering the years from 1922 through 1929, are the story of their marriage.

Although one reviewer forecast that this would not be a book for the many, but had very much to offer the few who were prepared to appreciate it, *Arnold* went through more editions and sold more copies than any other of Emilia Fogelklou's books. When she published it in 1944, as the war was entering its final catastrophic stage, she may well have wondered whether anyone would be interested in the tale of two highly intellectual, other-worldly, middle-aged lovers whose relationship was never once free of the shadow of disease and death. As she said in her preface, "But there is something in it that would venture out among people. The most serious reason for letting such a book as this go is perhaps just its untimeliness."[45] Because of its intensely personal and intimate content, Emilia seems originally to have intended that the work be published only after her death. Since that event did not occur until nearly three decades later, many had reason to thank her for sharing these experiences when she did. "It is the duty of extraordinary people," wrote another reviewer, "to tell the so-called ordinary ones about the possibilities life contains."[46]

Arnold is indeed a book about life's possibilities, particularly in the realm of the spirit. That so genuinely good a human being as Arnold Norlind could exist, that one could so harmoniously combine rigorous scholarship with literary artistry and mystical perception, that inexorable disease could be confronted by both the victim and his companion with such confidence and capacity for joy — these are among the central possibilities here affirmed. Unpleasant possibilities are not ignored — economic uncertainty, the physical misery of the sickroom, the oppressive sense of failure in finding one's true life calling, the weight of regret and guilt at not having understood or done what one might. The possibility and the reality of death are major themes in the work. In the concluding narrative chapter called "Afterward," Emilia Fogelklou relates something of her experiences of grief. Simply and unsensationally, she reveals the possibility of victory over grief in the insight, as Margit Abenius put it, that "what is essential in a person who has achieved clarity and maturity can influence and lead us after death."[47]

During the remainder of the 1940s, Emilia Fogelklou produced a number of shorter works that appeared in various periodicals and collecitons. Mention might be made of a lecture in English, "Quakerism and Democracy" (1949), which was her presidential address to the Friends Historical Society in London. Meanwhile, a friend put together an anthology of sixteen of Emilia's shorter compositions going back to 1905. It bore the title *Ljus finns ändå* (There is light still), words that were eventually to be inscribed over her grave.

While she was living in partial retirement in rural Sweden, she wrote the second of her three autobiographical books, *Bareheaded*. In logical order, this work constitutes the first part of her life story, beginning with her childhood and tracing her career to about 1921. As in the earlier work about her marriage, she wrote in the third person, calling herself by the family nickname "Mi." In addition to the narrative text, there are long quotations from her diaries and many passages from letters to her family and friends. The outward events of the book are not in themselves very remarkable. Yet, at a number of points the reader is gripped by the intensity of personal experience which is recorded. This intensity reaches its peak in the passages dealing with her time in Gothenburg and the overwhelming religious experience that came upon her at the age of twenty-three. How that event became the point of departure both for her subsequent academic and scholarly career and for her approach to life and other human beings is the substance of the rest of the book.

Four years after *Bareheaded*, Emilia Fogelklou published the third and last volume of her memoirs, entitled in Swedish *Resfärdig* (Ready to Travel). It contains the account of her life after Arnold Norlind's death in 1929 up to about 1951. The major events described are her two visits to America, her year at Woodbrooke, her wartime humanitarian activities, and the retreat to the country after 1946. The book concludes with her journey to Israel and Greece.

The author's subtle depth of insight is revealed in the cryptic titles she sometimes gave her books. *Bareheaded* conveys both an unwillingness to be stereotyped and perhaps also a certain direct exposure to the light, a certain vulnerability to life. *Ready to Travel* implies on one level the readiness to set out on assignments at the beckoning of an inner guide. But it also surely alludes to the figure of speech Arnold once used in a letter to Mi when she was away on a lecture tour: "Some other time I will be the captain out sailing the seas . . . . " The image occurs again in the moments just before his death.[48] That Arnold had traveled on ahead is the thought that forms the essential background for the whole book. Mi was ready to leave, but knew "she had lessons left to learn in the borderland before she got to travel further in."[49]

Ready to Travel did not receive the warm responses that almost universally acclaimed *Arnold* and welcomed *Bareheaded*. It contains factual errors and a great many small details that distract from the main narrative. Those who were Emilia's co-workers during the war sometimes found the account of their activities disappointing, perhaps just because in her humility she understated the dynamic role she herself had played. Certainly it is not a bright and happy book, even though it reflects moments of deep joy. In addition to the descriptions of illness and depression, even a near approach to death in the mid-thirties, there is the acutely painful story of the lost professorship and her intense effort to overcome a very understandable, but no less destructive, bitterness. In choosing passages from the work for inclusion here, I have selected several that depict these emotional struggles and the recurring experiences of inner healing, or, as Emilia put it, "the rays from the reality of love that kept poking holes in her despair."[50]

Despite its tone of finality, *Ready to Travel* was not to be Emilia Fogelklou's last book, except in the sense that it was the last that constituted a longer integral work. Aside from a new edition of *Birgitta* in 1955, there were three volumes of essays, lectures, and devotional pieces that appeared in the last two decades of her life. The titles are *Saints and Witches* (1952), *Form and Radiance* (1958), and *Remembered Images and Errands* (1963).

The topics taken up in these collections are often ones that the author had dealt with before and quite a few of the compositions had appeared elsewhere earlier. St. Birgitta was still a figure Emilia felt close to and fascinated by, as she was by medieval saints' legends and Meister Eckhart's sermons. She discussed psychology of witchcraft and the phenomenon of hatred. More fully than in previous works she gave consideration to art and artists, particularly to two twentieth-century Swedish painters, Carl Kylberg and Axel Erdmann. All through these three volumes there are numerous references to contemporary literature, not only that of Scandinavia, but of the other European lands. For a humanist by training, she exhibited a remarkable understanding, as the geologist Gunnar Beskow noted in a review, of the essential thought structures of contemporary natural science, especially in physics. Most of all, of course, her attention was devoted to religious and philosophical writers, and one is impressed by her ability to remain in contact with the thought of the postwar era even into her eighties.

In 1963, at eighty-five, she produced an article on the French critic and mystic, Georges Bataille, by no means an easily understood writer. She welcomed the new ecumenical spirit wholeheartedly, and, as always, she approached sympathetically all sorts of authors, Hindu and eastern, as well as Christian and western. Teilhard de Chardin, Martin Buber, Simone Weil, Hellmut Gollwitzer, Bede Griffiths, and Thomas Kelly are only some of the most frequently mentioned and quoted. As the literary historian Erik Hjalmar Linder said in an article in 1956, Emilia Fogelklou "is in touch with most of, and the best of, contemporary religious life."[51]

It is appropriate here to say something about the character and content of Emilia Fogelklou's writing in general. In the early years her literary style was the object of some criticism, since it often became heavy and complicated. Although her later writing achieved an admirable clarity and simplicity, some difficulties persisted. She could produce unconventional word combinations which are not only hard to translate with confidence, but can be unclear to Swedish readers as well. In both written and oral presentations, there was a tendency to move too rapidly from idea to idea without providing the necessary transitions. One critic explains this in terms of "an apparent difficulty in directing and controlling the strong waves of emotion that carried her forward."[52] In her finest work, however, a genuine artistry is revealed.

While she cannot be considered an important poet in the usual sense of the word, writing poetry was important to her, in part, perhaps, as a therapeutic exercise whereby she reached understanding of herself. A number of her poems are found in the autobiographical works, especially in *Arnold*. There the poem called "The Angels" is presented within a personal context that accentuates the meaning as a reflection of the inner struggle that accompanied the new friendship with Arnold Norlind and the prospects it contained. Nor is it surprising that her grief at his passing should become the source of other verse. The critic Sven Stolpe, who admitted he had little taste for most of Emilia Fogelklou's "lyrical attempts," also insisted that she had written "one great poem — in two lines."[53] He was referring to the mystical couplet she once sent to Arnold:

Jag vill ej vilja och ej icke-vilja.
Men viljas vill jag av mitt väsens Gud.[54]

I will not will and not not-will.
But I will be willed by my being's God.

The reader of Emilia Fogelklou's works soon begins to recognize certain key words that were essential in her attempt to speak of religious experience. These include reality, life, openness, boundlessness, and love. Like mystics in all ages, she made frequent use of the word *light*, and closely tied to it is the most important term of them all, *radiance (strålning).* Her profound personal experience at the age of twenty-three brought an overwhelming consciousness of Divine reality, which she perceived as radiant light, though she also speaks of goodness, joy and love. This radiance liberated and restored, and it also gave understanding from within, so that she could share life with others regardless of their views and opinions. For the rest of her days, she was less concerned with distinctions and lines of division than with what unifies, "the reality behind the interpretation and the radiance that came from that reality."[55]

"Yet it would be a mistake," writes Gunnel Vallquist in a most perceptive article,

> to think that in Emilia Fogelklou's view form and radiance are opposing concepts bearing negative and positive charges. Form, including religious dogma, is not something to be rejected, but something that must not become restrictive. It must be transcended, irradiated. Then it can itself acquire new meaning and radiant power . . . . In speaking of "true piety," she says that it neither questions nor obdurately defends formulations. "The spirit, radiance, is experienced within the accepted forms and clearly has its home in them, just as a person is at home in his native land or language."[56]

The idea of the form being penetrated by a radiant reality is not unrelated to Emilia Fogelklou's fondness for the word *tvärsigenom*. This may be translated "straight through"or "right on through" and stands in contrast to the evasive *udenom* or "round and about" of Ibsen's *Peer Gynt*. Once in a Quaker meeting for worship she is said to have stood up and repeated this pregnant word several times with such emphasis that some thought she was sneezing. In *right on through* there is the echo of her lifelong craving for genuineness and her commitment to obey the demands of her intellectual conscience. As a student she submitted her new-found certainty of Reality to the test of contradictory books, teachers and disciplines with an inner assurance that it would come through. For her, the term implied faith in the Reality that transcends barriers and opens up deeper, richer relationships with other human beings and with the whole of nature. It also meant facing the present and the future with confidence in the ultimate goodness of life — and death. She knew that to have broken through to a new consciousness of Reality was to find the source of courage to live fully one's own life.

> The courage to be oneself is the irreducible condition for real meaning in human action. But since to be oneself can only happen in one's own time, one must make a clear decision to will to live *in just this time*.[57]

Although Emilia Fogelklou may have thought it possible to withdraw into a quiet rural setting to live out the remainder of her days, the idea did not prove feasible. There were many calls upon her services, and it may well be that she did not really adjust to the more isolated situation. In the early 'fifties she moved to Lund and hoped that the small university town, which was filled with memories for her and where she had good friends, would provide both a comfortable environment and opportunities to work with young people. But after several years there, she decided to return to the estate at Högfors. In the early 'sixties she moved again, this time to the Stockholm suburb of Djursholm. Her final move, in 1966, was to Uppsala where she took up residence in a home for retired persons. There in July 1968, she celebrated her ninetieth birthday. Her last years were made more difficult by extreme deafness. She was still troubled by certain unhappy memories, and visitors found her conversation turning often to the disappointments of former years, especially the matter of the Uppsala professorship. In many ways she remained physically active, and an observer could be impressed by the vigor with which she strode along the Uppsala sidewalks.

Also impressive at her age was the continued strength of her intellectual and spiritual abilities. She was still an avid reader and quite willing to share what she learned with those who might be interested. In 1965 and 1966 she visited, among other places, a Danish teachers' college where Rigmor Fenger, an old friend from Woodbrooke days, was the *rektor*. Here Emilia talked with groups of students about recent archaeological discoveries in Sumeria and the evidence they yielded of an early matriarchal society. At another time, she interpreted for them Martin Buber's *I and Thou*, which had just appeared in Danish. She also spoke to the students about the significance of Pope John XXIII and the Second Vatican Council. Rigmor Fenger has written a lively description of her in this setting:

> After one such occasion, Emilia Fogelklou looked around the circle of young people and asked if they had any questions.
>
> "How is it to be so old?" one of them asked.
>
> The answer had an earnestness tinged with mischief.
>
> "Well, I'll tell you. I've gone to many kinds of schools, but of all the courses in the university of life, the course in old age is the hardest, the one with the most lessons to learn. Your own generation is gone. You can no longer count on your intellect or your memory. Your hearing lets you down. You can't keep track of things and you're constantly misplacing them. But you learn so much. You learn to accept help and to remember with your heart. To live always with the generations that went before, with those alive now, and with the generations to come — all that we must surely learn. In one way life is like a mountain climb, and we keep going steadily upward toward our death. And when we meet it, when Brother Death comes and gives us permission to go on across the frontier, then we must meet him with thankfulness, only with thankfulness."
>
> So it was that an eighty-eight-year-old sat with us and spoke with us, deaf though she was, but with a wonderful ability to grasp what was essential in the group's possibilities.
>
> Afterward I asked a student how it was to have so old a person as a teacher. "I felt so dull-witted," she said. "Emilia Fogelklou was the most alive of all of us and in a way the youngest, too. And so radiant!"[58]

A friend who visited her often in her last years noted how intensely she could experience everyday things in nature, like the tree in bloom outside her window. Visitors were sent away with a book from her library and when her books were all but gone, she gave them fruit or a flower. For those who she knew were in need, she was constant in prayer. "It usually helps, you know," she would say with a smile.

> How fervently she longed to die. "Hope to be out of school soon," was one of her frequent expressions. "But I suppose there is still something more I have to learn here," she would sigh. "Only the shell is left; most of me is already gone."[59]

In the summer of 1972, shortly after her ninety-fourth birthday, a severe fall and a broken hip necessitated her hospitalization. The two months of suffering inflicted upon her by the technical achievements of modern hospital care were a most painful conclusion to her long life. A devoted younger friend, Annie Jenhoff, has described this experience in a poignant article based on almost daily visits to Emilia's bedside. Hardly able to speak or hear, surrounded by the life-prolonging apparatus of medical science under the control of hospital personnel who knew virtually nothing about her and could not have cared less, Emilia Fogelklou again and again begged to be allowed "to go home." Instead, when her hip was declared to be sufficiently healed, she was moved, with unbelievable carelessness, to a convalescent hospital where the excruciating procedures to keep her alive were at first continued and then, on September 23, abandoned. On Tuesday, September 26, just four days before the fiftieth anniversary of her marriage to Arnold Norlind, she died. Heartrending though her account of Emilia's last weeks surely is, Annie Jenhoff beautifully describes several incidents in which those who came in contact with her were deeply affected. " . . . Mi influenced people to the very end just by existing, without words. The joy of coming within her circle of light and radiance I call *grace*."[60]

The death of Emilia Fogelklou occasioned an outpouring of appreciative articles in the Swedish daily press as well as in the journals identified with the causes for which she had worked. Gillis Hammar, himself eighty-five and one who had known both Emilia and Arnold over half a century before, wrote of her for the Uppsala paper. The large metropolitan newspapers all carried prominently placed accounts of her life by scholars, journalists, or friends. While most bore factual headlines or moderate assertions like "She spoke on behalf of the heart" or "A light has gone out in Swedish cultural life," one provincial paper announced the death with the words "Sweden's Only Saint" in large heavy letters. For this act of canonization it cited the authority of the controversial *litterateur* Sven Stolpe.[61] One can well imagine Emilia's discomfort had she seen this headline.

At the funeral service held under Quaker auspices in Djursholm Chapel on October 10, 1972, several moving tributes were offered by friends who had known her well in various connections, especially within the women's movement. Particularly touching were the words of the writer Barbro Alving who told of possessing a little book of Emilia Fogelklou.

> It is written by Emilia Fogelklou *literally*. It was not authored by her, but it is handwritten and there is only one single copy, mine. When she sat down to write it, she was seventy-eight years old.
>
> That was in 1956. Just after New Year's I was sentenced to the women's section of Långholm Prison to serve my month for refusing to do civil defense service. Compared to the lot of other political prisoners it was a trifling sentence, of course, but a month is a month, and I wasn't exactly accustomed to that sort of thing.
>
> Ili must have realized how it would be, that a month is a month and that the time might be heavy now and then. Words can help to brighten things, words that the inmate could get a foothold in, and God should be along in it too.
>
> There came in the mail a little notebook. Ili had thought of quotations and written them down in it on thirty pages, one or two selections for each of the thirty days, chosen from all sorts of literature of the kind that could give a confined, literally locked-in person the tools and the wings to get out through the bars.

Barbro Alving went on to give examples. They were from the wide range of Emilia Fogelklou's reading: from Oscar Wilde, Rilke, Victor Hugo, Walt Whitman, Spinoza, Shelley, St. Paul, and St. Francis. The Swedish hymnal and Swedish writers like Strindberg and Elin Wägner were represented, as well as a Chinese emperor and a country proverb from Skåne. There were lines by Arnold Norlind and a few of Emilia's own. "I know of no person, other than Emilia Fogelklou, who at seventy-eight, with such care, such thoughtfulness, in so spiritually *practical* a way, could show tenderness and concern for a fellow human being and friend."[62]

In the village of Västra Alstad in Skåne, Emilia Fogelkou lies buried beside her husband in the lovely little churchyard. On his stone are inscribed three lines from Dante's *Paradiso*; on hers, the three words: *Ljus finns ändå* — "There is light still."

BAREHEADED

"May I ask, sir, are you a Hat or a Cap?"

"Bareheaded," replied the stranger, placing his hand on his head, "preferably bareheaded, as the good Lord made me."

Heidenstam, *The Swedes and their Chieftains.*

Childhood and Youth

One secure place where Mi was always welcome was at her grandmother's. Since she had become blind, Grandma lived in an apartment in the basement. The high window with sills at ground level looked out upon the roadway. Down at Grandma's one could see all the feet and shoes and hoofs that passed by. It was a large room and contained Grandma's armchair, her bed, a chest of drawers, and a sofa, as well as a little shelf where she kept her devotional books. She knew by heart almost all the psalms in the Psalter and the hymns in the old hymnal.

It was a good place to be. Sitting there quietly with her knitting, Grandma had time for you, even when everyone else was busy and in a hurry. And seldom did she decline Mi's insistent offers to demonstrate her new skill in reading. Mi believed she was doing something exceptionally useful when she "read aloud to Grandma." In a childish voice, resounding with importance, she solemnly intoned the words. She showed a special liking for certain hymns that spoke of penitent sinners converted in the nick of time. Was it the forceful expressions that fascinated her? With delight she read about Sin:

> Down to earth he presses me,
> A load I cannot carry,
> So cruel and grim he seems to be,
> To death he would me harry.

Eventually Grandma suggested that Mi find a pleasanter hymn.

Mi knew very certainly that God was where Grandma was. There the atmosphere was different somehow.

When Mi was nine years old, Grandma died of typhoid fever. Except for a stolen glimpse when the door was ajar, Mi was unable to see her until she was laid out in her coffin with a white cap on her head and her hands folded across her breast.

It was never as easy to be sure about God anywhere else *indoors* as it had been at Grandma's.

But out of doors, with sky and sea and sunset, she could still know that God really existed. In such glories she could lose herself completely . . . .

It never occurred to her that what one learned in school had anything to do with the God who "took Grandma away." Nor did she perceive anything of it in church, where there was so much to look at: the ship-model that hung from the ceiling with billowing sails, or the little gilded figure of Moses which held up the heavy pulpit and the priest as well.

But *Easter* for her was something that had always been surrounded with light. Easter was a word associated with Grandma and the out-of-doors, the jubilant melody to the hymn "*Vad ljus över griften.*" It called to her mind a heavenly day in the garden. Long rows of spring flowers rising from the damp brown soil, the air full of sunlight and blue and loveliness and bright Sunday. Her two brothers sitting together on a bench by the summer-house carving willow whistles. And even before she thought of asking for one, Bie came forward in his sailor's blouse to present her with a fine whistle of her own to blow.

That day lay in a sort of celestial clarity beyond all wrangling and quarreling. Long afterward, that little scene flashed upon Mi's memory whenever she heard the words: "the whole earth be filled with His glory."

Anyone who has spent his childhood living next door to a windmill thinks of it as a friend. Even after it has fallen into armless decay, one can still hear its great swishing roar, for in the realm of memory it remains alive.

Inside the mill there lay a world of exciting possibilities. The miller's boy could let you ride on the chain-hoist and, either alone or in the company of a sack of flour, journey all the way to the top or down to the bottom. Lying on your back you discovered new lighting effects and movements. The flour dust danced in the sunlight. Restless flickering shadows played upon the floor like strange swift birds when the millvanes whisked past outside the little windows. Everything that had once been grey or brown or black or red was frosted over with a soft layer of flour. Far off in the corners the spider webs were powdered white.

Even when the wind was still, the whole structure trembled as the hoist rattled its way up to the top or down to the base of the mill. Down there it was dark as night when the door to the road was closed.

While the vanes roared outside, one was surrounded with creaking and rumbling and shaking. If the wind were not blowing too hard, it was possible to go out on a balcony on the revolvable top of the mill. From here one could look out over the whole world — the rolling plain of Österlen, the ancient burial mounds, the farms, the wheeling flocks of birds and the sea. But from the balcony one could not investigate the secrets of the vanes, for they were always on the other side. No, to get nearer to them you had to press yourself ever so tightly to the outside wall of the mill and crawl as close as you dared to the mighty rushing hurricane. The strong blast of air whirled and whipped right through your little body, making it shiver with both fear and delight.

She dreamed often of being carried away by one of the great wings. It looked so simple to seize hold of the wooden grillwork under the sail and so be whisked outward far beyond the vanes themselves till one landed upon another star. How would you come back again? Perhaps you never would. Instead you would just fly directly to heaven and have much more to see than from the balcony — and maybe say hello to Grandma.

These fantasies provided many exciting adventures, most of them just within oneself, of course. But anyone who had been touched by the magic of the millvanes could never remain completely quiet about those daring journeys.

Once Mi was invited to visit the doctor's three little girls in town. They were almost the same age as she, but they had never had a windmill for a friend. She was enthusiastically recounting one imaginary journey after the other when the girls' mother chanced to come in. She gave the little narrator a reproachful glance and said, somewhat sharply, "All that is just *not true*."

It remained a painfully unpleasant memory, a pang of humiliation which caused Mi to seem ignominious in her own eyes, to feel inferior, and to brood.

She could not remember any other time in her childhood when she had lied. Was that a "lie"?

All those mill fantasies collapsed like an empty bubble . . . . After that blow she could not remember anything more about the mill. It destroyed her naive experience of the world of fantasy. Were there two kinds of "real"? And can only the one kind be called true? Must the gates be shut upon one world in order to live properly and rightly in the other?

Not long afterward the mill vanes did take someone away. The neighbors' little four-year-old Johanna did not return from her heavenly journey, but was buried in a grave down in the earth. They said she got too close to the sails.

The mill served as a useful member of society in that world which people thought of as real. It ground the flour for daily bread. But Mi believed it was something more, as well. It was a world full of strange secrets, sometimes flitting softly and merrily like flour dust in the sunbeams, sometimes booming like the roar of a storm, sometimes casting the black-armed shadows of death. People took the one world into account. But what of the other one? Why didn't they talk about that? She grew shy of her winged friend.

A sword of truth had driven her out of that paradise.

But there were other things. There was the iridescent play of the evening sun. Mi would hang on the gate by the road and lose herself in endless beholding. A long time she could cling there, deaf to all summons. Something within her trembled and sang. But not aloud. Far beyond the great burial mound lay a white farmstead amid spreading trees. She peopled it with noble beings. She often watched the swallows flying in that direction in the evening light.

From the same gate she got to see the wonder of a mirage. It appeared in the morning. The horizon opened up and one saw not only the sky against the sea, but a whole long row of upside-down ships, their masts and sails visible with a peculiar sharpness. Perhaps it was the sailing fleet from Åland. They were transparently clear in the surrounding sunlight. Something vibrated within her as when a bow is drawn across the strings. If only the vision would never disappear. Think of having the whole world upside down! Though her weight was cracking one of the gate-slats beneath her feet, she stood there until the vision was completely gone.

"Mirage," it was called. Many people could see it at the same time. It was no fantasy. So many kinds of reality there were!

She could never afterward accept the expression "only a mirage." That was said by people who had never seen one. It was just as real, even if no one saw it . . . .

Mi was not prepared for the new sister who burst in upon her kingdom. People in a large family did not as yet pay heed to psychological risks involved in such a situation. She seems to have reacted with unusual violence in this crisis of deposition. She suffered from an inflammation of the stomach, became irritable, and fell into tantrums without anyone understanding the cause. Her hair straightened and lost its lustre. Like those who have been pushed aside, she wanted most to flee to some hiding place. Sometimes she would come rushing up and cry, "Hold me, Mother," only to pull away immediately and return to her solitary games. Her hostility toward her dolls . . . and that preference for more drastic hymn verses were perhaps related to her dethronement . . . .

She was now sure she was a foundling about which she had read in the fairy tales. Perhaps she never had belonged to the family. The notion grew and grew. And so one day she got out her dead grandmother's brown shawl with the white silk edges. She tied it on and, enveloped in Grandma, set out to seek her fortune in the great wide world.

She can have been scarcely ten years old when she made up her mind to leave for good. In the wind and rain, she sat down to rest in a ditch a couple of miles from home. She was hungry and crying when the beloved Tilda, the family cook and general mainstay, found her and cajoled her into returning home. "Nobody misses me, Tilda, nobody." But Tilda's powers of love were great. She and hunger and discomfort in the ditch on that windy autumn day brought the fugitive home again . . . .

Mi's father was appointed district clerk for a subdivision of the province. Now the family could live in the provincial capital where there were more advanced schools. This was indeed fortunate, since the expense of boarding out two of the older children had made deep inroads into the family resources.

And so they moved. No more sea, no more mirages, no more garden or sunsets or hilltops from which to look out over the great wide world. Now they lived on a street, and when one looked out of the windows there was only another stone building to rest one's eyes upon. How peculiar it felt to breathe without inhaling that whiff of salt and sea. Mi's head felt strange, drawing in the empty air. It was as if one's nose didn't *get* anything. She had always disliked bad odors, but this was nothing at all, good or bad, she thought. Just emptiness, emptiness.

The formal moving took place in October, but the "little" girls had to take the school entrance examinations the previous spring. They had expected Mi, who was twelve, to be easily admitted to the Fifth Class and Gerd to be accepted into the Second. But just to be sure, Gerd was tested for Third and made it, while Mi, who was feeling lost in the strange air and town, and a bit afraid of the new teachers, ended up in a lower class than was anticipated.

And yet school work was the only thing she had really succeeded at, her only kingdom. The twelve-year-old girl was seized with a terrible despair, sharpened naturally by earlier experiences, although no one understood it at the time. She felt as though everything was dying out. She fainted, had stiffness in her limbs, and became actually sick with despondency. To make matters worse, Mother was at home at Backen during the examination time and the following summer. Father, extremely busy getting adjusted to his new work, could only call in a doctor. But the doctor was a complete stranger. To the twelve-year-old it seemed the end of the road, death's door.

Mi could remember how she thought about the daughter of Jairus, also twelve years old. She had, however, been raised from the dead, and around her bier people had stood grieving and lamenting, whereas Mi had to die all alone with no one to come and restore her to life. So hard had the disappointment struck that she found no comfort in being moved up to the Fifth Class the following Christmas. That achievement never really meant anything. What was supposed to be "childhood's self-evident sense of security" had been dealt another cruel blow. She had lost faith in her own capability. Grandma was dead, and Nature, the *real* Nature of countryside and sea, was inaccessible in this new town.

Yet she was the child of a stable marriage and continued to have happy moments. But whenever she later tried to recall her childhood, it was the distinct rhythms of death and renewal that came to mind with greatest clarity.

The deadly blow to all her self-confidence, coming at the age of twelve, proved a significant turning point. She felt that the foundation of her life had been shaken just when she was in her most sensitive years . . . .

One of her new schoolmates, Helga Fick . . . lived in the country near Vanås Castle, which contained a famous gallery of paintings. Mi spent the Easter holiday with Helga and was given access to the collection of pictures. She could go and look at them as long as she wished, not just glance over them hastily. There were old Dutch masters and works from the Cologne school, as well as Italian paintings. Mi had never before seen art of this high quality. At home there were only reproductions, oleographs, or amateur sketches from Bornholm and the like. Therefore, the first encounter with genuine art made an overwhelming impression upon her. Mi lived in the paintings, dreamed about them. From certain of them something alive streamed out over her. Her mind was so deeply agitated that she lay sleepless the first night. It was a completely new kind of reality she had encountered . . . .

Mi was two years younger than her dearest classmates. They were to start confirmation instruction in the Seventh Class, but Mi's parents considered her too young and thought it would be more suitable for her to finish the Eighth Class first and then have her confirmation instruction during a quieter year. As a result, there was a great deal which her classmates had in common which lay outside Mi's world. The old disease of feeling excluded returned, and this happened just at that sensitive time around the onset of menstruation. One of her older sisters explained its implications to her and tried to help her, but, as far as she was concerned, the whole process seemed superfluous since she had no intention of ever getting married — if indeed anyone would ever want the family's ugliest daughter for a wife.

Up in the attic stood an enormous double bed made of light birch, inlaid with narrow winding strips of darker wood. It served as a storage place for spare rugs and other pieces of cloth . . . . Here Mi found a hideaway where she could read by the daylight that filtered through a small dusty window. Out of sight and away from other people, she could also write down her secret thoughts in a square yellow notebook.

In a pile of old books in the corner of the attic she one day came upon a copy of Bjursten's *Reader*. In her secret place she opened it at random and read the poem "On Genius" by Johan Henrik Kjellgren. Like a sudden revelation, the meaning of the poem struck her with complete clarity. The words, which became etched upon her memory, went as follows: "Do you feel your blood catch fire, your heartbeat quicken . . . . at that which leaves another quite unmoved? Then, noble one, attend the divine voice of genius! Be great — and unhappy!" With tears streaming down her cheeks and an intense excitement coursing through her limbs and very marrow, Mi copied the words into her secret book in large, childish handwriting.

Whenever the other children had made fun of her physical reactions to injustice or beauty or goodness, had not Mother told them, "Let her alone. She can't help it that she has such a burning heart." The nickname "The Burning Heart" that her brothers had called her after that now had a lofty and compensatory explanation! Now she no longer cared that her schoolmates were taking the confirmation class with the pastor.

The teenage girl had experienced a secret initiation. Where it would lead, she had no idea. Would she perhaps even write books some day? Or what? Her heart beat violently as she lay there among the spare rugs, shaking with sobs. Was that the way she would become great? Was that how she was going to be unhappy?

In the course of church history at school, they came to the post-reformation sects, which were usually treated unsympathetically in Hildebrand's textbook. Eventually they reached George Fox, the Quaker, whose delusion was believing that one could be led by *the Inner Light*. "That's my delusion, too," said Mi out loud in class. The teacher, however, took no notice of it. Mi may have known very little about the Quakers, but she meant seriously what she said. All the important things happened inside you — of that she was already completely convinced.

At sixteen, and after finishing her regular schooling, Mi began taking her confirmation instruction. By that time, her older brothers and sisters had already formed their opinions about life . . . . The young people might discuss matters forcefully at times, but it never occurred to anyone to try to impose his views on someone else. The atmosphere was altogether too free. As she moved among them, Mi was becoming aware that they and she were all surrounded by the common mantle of their parents' affection, a tenderness that was fresh and wholesome, rarely sentimental, more often tinged by a bit of humor.

This freedom and affection was accompanied by a certain reluctance to guide or plan for the children. They had to venture out and find their own way. Yet Fej's periodic bouts with asthma, Nan's sometimes clumsy missionary efforts, and the younger brother's bohemian associations, as well as the economic difficulties of the time, left a troubled impression on Mi's teenage years.

She ought to have taken confirmation instruction earlier. The handsome, kind and simple pastor explained Christ's presence in the Eucharist by saying that God was everywhere. She felt unhappy, since she thought she already knew all that by heart and that it was terribly boring, which, of course, was sinful even to think. She was also too immature to understand what it was all about when one of the girls in the confirmation class became pregnant and the pastor began several lessons in a row by strangely intoning, in an almost liturgical fashion: "Remember now that the sin of fornication is such a nasty sin."

It was clear to her that she was completely "unworthy and unfit" to receive communion. She lay awake at night and thought about how she might declare that she had no right to promise anything. She was not at all sure what she did and did not believe of the Christian doctrine. But she understood how much unhappiness it would cause at home if, on top of the asthma, the decision about the missionary career, and the bohemian friends, she should distress her parents by refusing to be confirmed — something that no one had ever done in their town.

She said nothing to her mother, but night after night she prayed ardently for an honest way out. And, indeed, just before the crucial day, she found help from the passage in the Catechism about "The Forgiveness of Sins, Life and Blessedness." Here was the answer to her doubts about the meaning of belief: "It is to covet with all one's heart what these words promise." She certainly knew that she coveted that. Now she would not have to make her father and mother unhappy. She could go forward in that kind of faith.

Sunday came. There were so many children to be confirmed that they filled the whole railing, and Mi, who was the last one in line, had to wait and stand alone, looking on. Then a lady quite unknown to Mi came up to her and embraced the solitary child. And when it was Mi's turn, it was Dean Flygare who, with full intensity of heart, laid his hand on her head and spoke the words with such warmth and personal meaning that long afterward she could hear them in his bright and fervent voice ". . . . keep thee for time everlasting."

The Breakthrough

(Note: In 1899 Emilia Fogelklou completed her training at the Teachers College in Stockholm and graduated with honors. Her first job began the following autumn at an elementary girls school in Landskrona, not far from her home. In the summer of 1900 a friend lent her a copy of Harnack's *What is Christianity*?)

The lender of the book had expected Mi to respond in long letters filled with anxiety over this new way of critically approaching the Bible. But when the reactions were quite the opposite, she recommended Mi in place of herself for a job in a new progressive school.

Mi received a letter offering her the position and describing the ideas which were to govern the new school. She was thrilled by them. But on the last page of the letter came the sentence: "We are thinking of assigning to you the classes in religion."

To be sure, it was in the lower grades, but Mi understood in her very bones that she was not ready for such a task in a pioneer school. She could not, therefore, accept the offer, although it would have meant a somewhat higher salary and, above all, the excitement of having a part in a creative undertaking.

Nevertheless, the episode gave the young teacher a powerful boost. She had thought of herself as so incompetent, so inexperienced and immature. She had a sort of religious faith, but mostly at second hand and altogether too shallow and vague to enable her to teach religion on her own.

Although she had turned the opportunity down, the position at the new school in Gothenburg was offered to her again sometime later, and she accepted it. Only after she had actually arrived did she learn that she would have to teach the classes in religion in the lower grades. Every one of those classes and each of the morning devotions caused her inward distress and struggle, for her self-imposed standard of complete truthfulness had grown ever more demanding.

The headmaster of the school, Artur Bendixson, opened up new vistas for school and community. He welcomed "the world's youngest faculty" with the statement: "I do not expect you to have the same opinions as myself. But I do expect every one of you to have a real opinion of your own about the things that are important here." And he continued, "In this school, children are, first of all, children, and then after that, they are schoolchildren. And those of us who teach here are, first of all, people, and then after that, school people. It is your job, together with the children, to create the spirit of this school."

Mi was completely captivated by the ideal of school and community they were trying to realize. It was fresh and vital, in contrast to the old worn routines. It was as if they had no ready-made pattern of behavior, clearly outlined once and for all, never to be critically examined. In every situation one had to work one's way through to a valid solution of a child's problem, then and there. Mi understood how important it was for her not to leap at new ideas just because they were right for other people, but instead to hold to what was really true for herself. She wanted to be absolutely "on the level," especially when it came to teaching the most difficult material. The headmaster, a man of Jewish background, was brilliant, warmhearted, and deeply sensitive. Mi's feminine colleagues were attractive young women and the men were good companions.

The school had the reputation of being very "dangerous," and how much these young people enjoyed being thought dangerous! And how much they labored overtime, as if it were their greatest pleasure! Mi wrote out her lessons on a cyclostyle, a messy duplicating device. They visited in each other's homes as welcome guests. Teachers and pupils were like one big family. Sometimes they borrowed a farm for a week of studying botany or practicing housekeeping. And during the "free period," the janitor, who had been a diver, sat with them at the big round table and told stories of life at the bottom of the sea. Mi was living with all her lives, and work, too, was fun.

Most meaningful of all was the headmaster, this gifted person who was so different from everyone else in the demands he made, in his goodness, and in his paradoxical way of speaking. He often came into the classroom and spoke with the children. Once he came to Mi's class carrying a handful of yellow roses and chatted with the children about their assignments. A little girl spoke up and asked, "Now can we give you an assignment, Mister Headmaster?"

"What do you want me to do?" he inquired.

"Well, learn by heart what is written there on the blackboard," she replied. From the preceding class there remained the words, "Blessed are the poor in spirit, for they shall see God." The headmaster promised and left.

The next day he came into the classroom and recited these words with such calm warmth and solemnity that the children sat silently for a time after he had quietly disappeared.

Within herself Mi was constantly struggling with questions about how to teach religion and maintain complete honesty about what was valid and definite. Having no one with whom she could talk things out, she had to find solid ground on her own. She felt that there must be a way to reach *Reality* — if there was any such thing at all, if everything were not mere subjectivity. It had nothing to do with the then current question of Biblical criticism or the differences between Harnach and the traditional believers. All that was of little interest to her.

Despite her limited experience of living, she was absolutely clear that the question she was struggling with — that of the reality or unreality of God — concerned nothing less than the whole of life, its value, its nature and its direction. (Though it never occurred to her at the time, she later reflected that her grandparents' fervent piety and her mother's intellectual crisis on entering a new era might have exerted an influence upon her, along with the fact that she alone of the regular members of the faculty had been assigned to teach religion.) It all became immense and overpowering for the lonely little person.

There came moments when she was seized with despair.

Would she ever be able to stay on? And yet there was nowhere else she would rather be. "Never acquire your own honor or happiness at the cost of sorrow for the least of your fellows," her father had once written. But the more seriously she took her responsibilities in teaching religion, the more she found discomfort, conflict and sorrow over it. The others considered her all too "Christian," whereas that was just what she was not, as she herself well knew.

"You are necessary to this school. But on this point there will inevitably be conflict between us," the headmaster had said, and his words rang in her ears.

One rainy spring evening, she felt so lonely and hopeless that she walked and walked, far out of her way along the river. She remembered the prayer that had been constantly on her lips as a fourteen-year-old: "God, let me not have to live." It seemed such an easy leap from here; one *could* escape. If you really wanted to. The water didn't look so forbidding.

At just that moment she had the strange feeling that her mother and father were present with her. She saw them just as they used to be at home, sitting at the round table. She felt that, for herself, she hadn't the slightest satisfaction in staying here. But if she left, she would cause them pain, shame, gloom, questions — as well as loss.

She turned toward home sobbing. Hadn't she just recently told the children at morning devotions that sometimes you have to do what you don't want to, simply because it is right?

During the next few days her work was performed in a peculiar dream-like fashion. She could scarcely believe that people accepted her as real, accepted her responses as real. She knew better than they that she was just a shell, a shell empty of life. If only she could have felt a sense of guilt! The pure nothingness was worse. She didn't even exist. It was as if she'd never been at all.

But then one bright spring day — it was the 29th of May, 1902 — while she sat preparing for her class under the trees in the backyard at Föreningsgatan 6, quietly, invisibly, there occurred the central event of her whole life. Without visions or the sound of speech or human mediation, in exceptionally wide-awake consciousness, she experienced the great releasing inward wonder. It was as if the "empty shell" burst. All the weight and agony, all the feeling of unreality, dropped away. She perceived living goodness, joy, light like a clear, irradiating, uplifting, enfolding, unequivocal reality from deep inside. The first words which came to her — although they took a long time to come — was, "This is the great Mercifulness. This is God. Nothing else is so *real* as this." The child who had cried out in anguish and been silenced had now come inside the gates of Light. She had been delivered by a love that is greater than any human love.

Struck dumb, amazed, she went quietly to her class, wondering that no one noticed that something had happened to her.

"Ye must be born again," it says in the New Testament. And that was just what had happened to her. But the experience was too overpowering for her to be able to find words for it. It was over a year before she could speak of it with anyone else. The only indication she gave was during an errand to the school office, when she remarked quietly, as if in passing, "Now I'm through." More was not needed.

She experienced a new freedom, a new healthiness. It was as if a restrictive husk had fallen off, and not only from herself but from others as well. In a new way she could now see through the veils of others, both when she met people and when she read books. Fearfulness disappeared. Within herself she *knew*, without priest or book, how God finds a person and bestows life and freedom and light. The New Testament opened up from within. She understood that what had happened to her was possible for *everyone*. It was part of human life. She recognized glimpses of it in the churches and the sects, but for herself she did not require so much "wrapping paper around God," not so many repetitions of the same thoughts and words, as if God were deaf or forgetful or reluctant to listen. Silence concealed less. To discover the Reality in other beings was also a form of revelation.

She felt compelled to learn more about those who had consciously had the same experience. She read the mystics and began to think about studying theology for this very purpose. Yet all around her she encountered the view that "religious experience" is a subjective illusion. Therefore, she had to verify her experience in the light of just that philosophy and psychology which did *not* take into account any religious Reality. She must subject herself to that acid test. For if such studies could destroy her strong perception of the Reality, then it did not pass the test. (In her heart, of course, she was sure it would pass!) But she saw before her a long and difficult course of studies in the two areas. For the time being, she applied for admission to the Institute of Philosophy and Sociology. Theological studies would have to be postponed to the future. Psychology she worked through on her own.

During the days when the transformation took place within her, she frequently experienced the sort of minor miracles usually only written about in legends. For a time she lived so brightly and happily alert that she couldn't fall asleep before dawn. Yet several mornings in a row, a bumble bee flew in at the open window and waked her at the right time, like an alarm clock! People whom she had thought to visit came to her of their own accord. The whole long school day was studded with sparkling, happy little miracles. Trees, flowers and clouds unfolded their beauty in a new way. Everything that lived acquired a multiplicity of lives.

In this period she ceased to worry about the opinions and views of other people, and yet she felt a new sharing of life with everyone. She met others from the inside, including her colleagues, who had no notion of what she had experienced.

Was this not to have gained "the life which is life indeed"? Neither church, nor priest, nor Bible had converted her. It was the living spirit of God that had come down into the lifeless being, so that she finally knew what Life is and what Love is, without that knowledge being bound to any outward intermediary. She saw that we all belong indissolubly together in the depths of God. Christ knew this, lived this, found this among publicans and sinners. She stood before an inexhaustible well of new thoughts, feelings and certainties. The richness was too overwhelming for her to be able to draw up more than a few drops at a time. She was boundlessly happy.

Her talent for mathematics seemed gradually to be dissipated in a strange way. Perhaps the new reality, rising from secret springs, took away her interest. Logical reasoning about religion became quite foreign to her. Views and opinions were no longer of concern. Now it was the reality behind the interpretation, and the radiance that came from that reality, which mattered.

What she had experienced within herself became decisive for her life.

Nothing drove her out into the streets and byways to issue proclamations. She knew confidently that the Reality is waiting for all. But to acquire more and more insight into this life, that was what she must do, so that she could help build bridges between the worlds of men. For was that not what people needed *now*? That was precisely why she had to test the new life against what opposed and denied it. That was why she must study, not to acquire certainty, but to test certainty.

During the summer she read Haeckel and Pfister and Nietzsche. But with help from Robertson-Smith and Wellhausen, she most of all read the prophets and *lived* in them. In exultation she walked, or rather sped, along the highways as if she were above time and space. Late one evening on such a walk, she saw the moonbeams playing upon a meadow near the sea, where there grew great clusters of blue sandbells. All of them were alive. And it was as if her breast would burst with the blessed beauty of these fellow creatures.

She had not yet had time to venture out into action. She was simply incomprehensibly happy. People thought she had become secretly engaged. They said she was radiant. And she smiled at that. She had indeed leapt beyond everything that had to do with engagements and was at home in a love that would irradiate all!

For the most part, she lived in this sense of elevation through the years of her youth, when most are normally attracted to the opposite sex. There were men who were fond of her, but they understood that she was borne by another wave than the one they could lift her into. That she was homely she completely forgot. She simply lived. And everything around her, even the ugly, the mean and the difficult, had another life to anticipate beyond the wrappings and the shell. "Blessed are the poor in spirit" is not a phrase to be repeated, but a truth to be experienced.

Years of Study

(Note: In 1905, Emilia Fogelklou left the school in Gothenburg, having been given a generous fellowship for further studies at the university.)

She traveled to Uppsala to consult Nathan Söderblom about entering upon her studies at the beginning of the next term. That she should start with the history of religion in the Philosophical Faculty was already clear in her mind.

She happened to come on just the day when the Söderbloms held their reception for students. Nevertheless, she had an opportunity to discuss her plans. She gave him to understand that she had to study these subjects because of a profound inner experience and not with any thought of a clerical office. She wanted to know if he considered it a *Christian* experience, since she had not had any specific consciousness of the person of Christ or of any particular New Testament words, and yet had indeed experienced a breakthrough in the life of the spirit which made the prophets and the New Testament meaningful to her as never before . . . .

The professor said that he could prove to her that an experience such as she described could occur only within the framework of Christian piety. He would demonstrate this to her later; for the time being she would have to trust him.

Oddly enough, there exists a description, written by another person who was present that same evening. Greta Beckius, who was then studying theology and philosophy, wrote, in her unpublished novel of Uppsala life, entitled *Marit Grene:*

> One dark autumn evening, while the rain pelted down and a stiff wind blew, Marit made her way with a friend out to attend the reception held each week by one of the theology professors for his students.
>
> In a small white room with many pictures on the walls sat several people. On the sofa were the professor and a young woman who seemed to be the center of attention in the company. Marit sat down shyly on a chair near the door to watch and listen to what was taking place.
>
> Beneath his blond wavy hair, the professor's face was bright and lively as his blue eyes were fixed with keen interest upon the young woman who sat beside him. She was just then telling a story with a voice and gestures in which every nuance of what she was saying was immediately reflected, so immediately indeed, that Marit, in her inhibited shyness, was almost shocked.
>
> "Why, she is almost making a racket," thought Marit.
>
> But the young woman could also become very quiet as she listened attentively. Her grey-blue eyes had a strange look, as if they gazed off into another world above her, someplace high and broad and luminous, where she would gladly have tarried . . . .

It was part of Mi's theological course requirement to attend a seminar on the New Testament. It took up the matter of the virgin birth. Mi was the only woman in the group. It became more and more uncomfortable to be present as the old-fashioned orthodox presentation went forward. She experienced a dreadful nausea each time she had to attend. It was her belief, at least, that it resulted from the abstruse way of approaching the whole subject, not as an aspect of the history of religion, but rather as a kind of dogmatic man-talk.

An old theology professor with sideburns lived in the same house. One day when Mi was returning home from the unpleasant seminar, she met his kindly wife on the stairs. And when the old lady, with some anxiety in her voice, asked how she was, Mi blurted out her disgust and despair at what she had just come from.

The next day, just as Mi's roommate was holding a little party for her brother and a couple of his fellow law students, the professor came up and knocked on the door. He wanted to see Mi. The party moved quickly to another room, while the professor, a broad smile on his face and two heavy books under his arm, sat himself down on the red and white striped sofa. He had heard from his wife that Mi was having trouble with the question of the virgin birth, and he had come to clear away all the difficulties. He opened up his encyclopedias to several articles on parthenogenesis in animals and humans. He read aloud, sermonized, expounded, greatly satisfied with himself at being able so easily to remove all obstacles.

It became so quiet in the next room, where earlier there had been talking and laughter. Mi was filled with indignation. She was ready to throw the well-meaning old man out. His exposition struck her as strange and repulsive. Finally he left. The company in the next room looked terribly amused. How much they had heard she did not know. The kindly old fellow would doubtless not have objected to letting his brilliance shine over all of them as well!

Mi developed a high fever, and a couple of days later was in the hospital with an advanced case of appendicitis. Whatever the price, she experienced a blessed relief at getting out of that seminar. She couldn't help feeling that it had been the cause of her illness, no matter how unreasonable the coincidence might appear. (In contrast, the study of Hebrew and the Old Testament were particularly meaningful for her, as is made clear in passages from her diary.)

How much I have gained from reading the Yahweh songs in Isaiah, especially the 53rd chapter! Never did they so grip me as in the original Hebrew version. They have *etched* their image into me. What I have managed to *preserve* is the image they have given to my soul, but not the expression and the explanation through which the life of the image must have been communicated.

To read part of the pronouncements of the prophets *in Hebrew* made them several degrees more real and immediate. There stood the man — there, the living God — over there, the message. They were contemporary. They had a *here* — and — *now quality, and they were demanding*.

Mi trembled in body and mind as she came to understand their disturbing seriousness.

And the figure of Jesus became far more real and understandable when she could place him in the context of the succession of prophets. His message was universal and yet personal. But one destroys the vital connection with human beings by forcing him into ancient mythical notions about the virgin birth.

What seemed most appropriate of all to her was the way the primitive church placed far more emphasis on celebrating the baptism of Jesus, the moment when he experienced being "born of God." It did not worry her that this was heresy. She had never intended to become a priest in the "Royal Swedish State Church." What she sought from all her studies was clarity about the great Reality she had experienced.

> 6 November 1908. The important thing for me is not the elucidation of theories, but rather great faith, apart from formulae and ritual. The discovery of God within each and every person, the blasting away of all the mountains of prejudice and everything else that gets in the way of experience of Him. I can understand well enough how it may be important to wipe the soot from the lenses of the telescopes available to us, but it is even more important to get rid of the dregs of mistrust that blur our vision of the possibilities in others and their consciences. Yet no one ought or can really act according to the conscience of someone else. Even if others have progressed much farther, an imitation is unacceptable to God . . . .

There came a telephone call. Would Mi perhaps go to see Gerda Norlander, her sick school friend, right away, since no one else could be at home with her? "I am just going out on my way to the dentist," Mi replied. But then, for some unexplained reason, she immediately added, "But I'll call and cancel the appointment." And she did.

Gerda was suffering from heart disease and was sitting in an armchair, propped up by many pillows. Her breathing was labored. But her expression was deep and peaceful. Beneath the dark hair, her thin face was colored by an intense spot of red on each cheek. She asked Mi to read something aloud. Mi did so. Then it seemed as if the invalid wanted to change her position. She leaned her back against Mi's breast and said, "No matter what I do, you must be still." Mi was completely still. It looked as if Gerda had fallen asleep. She breathed much more slowly. And Mi did not stir from the spot. Everything was strangely exalted. All time disappeared.

There was no fear. She sensed that it was as if a moth flew out of its cocoon. Something great and bright and calm and clear.

Had hours or minutes passed? Mi did not know. She sat still without moving. The housekeeper came in from the hall and suddenly screamed, "But good God — she's *dead*!"

Mi went home. That night she had a strange experience. Gerda had indeed died in her arms, without Mi knowing that it was death. Several hours later, in the stillness of night, consciousness awoke in the nerves against which the figure rested. Now Mi perceived with bodily awareness the stiffening, the cooling, the physiological side of the dying. It made a deep impression.

It was Mi's very first direct meeting with Brother Death. And it was totally free of fear — great, free and open.

(In early 1911 Emilia Fogelklou traveled to Italy to continue her studies. Her diary account contains the following passages:)

> In Venice, after a fresh spell of loneliness, I was able to take part like a child in the jubilant celebration of Italy's fiftieth anniversary with all this Italian capacity for enjoying "una festa."
>
> The music reaches me from the piazza. Up here in this bell-tower *pension* I am sitting far above the hum and celebration, which will go on all night.
>
> The shutters are closed. But still I know how it all looks, how the facade of San Marco is illuminated, how the crowd mills happily about, once the pigeons have been shooed out of the way.
>
> The room here is terribly filled with mirrors. I have to see myself multiplied many times in my white sweater, a little spot tossing on the waves of the humming sound. If only I were pretty, or intellectual! But Thou hast made me the *very most ordinary person* — in appearance, manners, reactions. Never, save when Thou wilt, does an ounce of life radiate from me.
>
> All the while I hear the music from San Marco and see the gladness and wonder down below.
>
> Is it Thy will that I should be released from all bonds?
> I know of nothing on earth I want . . . .
>
> "I don't know anyone as lonely as you are!" the headmaster once said to me in Gothenburg. But what was that then, compared to now, after all I've left behind along the way?

Loneliness is nothing noble,
nothing peculiar to you.
It is the most ordinary thing in the world.

From it links should
be firmly joined
with all lonely beings on the earth.

Thus from loneliness's fellow feeling
life is born.
Thus God takes shape,

He alone belongs to all.
And you lose yourself to them,
Give away your soul in prayer for all the
lonely of the whole wide world.

Strangely enough, it was not painting that I most appreciated in Venice, but architecture — the courtyards, the wells, the bridges, the play of sunlight and shadow over all of it. Wandered along the shore of the Lido and sat a long time in the Jewish cemetery. While I sat there a new light was suddenly thrown over my own past life.

A child I was. About myself I knew nothing.
Thou met me. Thou came and found my soul.
Thou saw. Then I saw too. I knew who I was.
And who Thou wert. But the hidden laws
uniting our beings, we could not freely behold.

And I was still a child,
not even a maid. And far from a grown woman.
Did not even understand that the flame consumed,
that it took my youth.
I merely felt in joy that I existed.
My young glow was carried in to where all find room —
and where none is lonely, though he walks alone.

ARNOLD

Friendship in the Dante-World

Christmas arrived in 1914 at an old home from which the children had long ago flown. They had usually come back for the holidays with their spouses and little ones. But this Christmas it was only the unmarried daughter, a school teacher from out of town, who would be accommodated, for the old father had been told that he had an advanced case of cancer which no doctor could cure.

He was past seventy. The world seemed to him darker than ever before, now that the war was revealing a cancer worse than his own. He could no longer become irascible. He still walked about a little in his room, but it was no longer a cloud of pipe smoke but one of gloom that threw its shadow around him . . . .

His wife — "Mother," he usually called her — could not accept inevitable things. Life and death were not decided by doctors, and that dreadful war would certainly come to an end soon, and even so, one certainly ought to remember it was Christmas, she thought. She worked with arrangements for the holidays as she had in years past. But to herself she sighed with longing for the grandchildren or perhaps simply for something resembling festivity and cheer.

And the daughter? Even before Mi had arrived home and found out what ailed her father, she had been depressed. How much her depression came from her feelings about what was happening out there in the world and how much of it was a matter of personal relationships, she couldn't tell. But the bubbling happiness she had always taken in her work before had somehow disappeared. "We three old people," she wrote in a letter to her sisters that Christmas.

With a weary indifference Mi had gone through a large packet of Christmas mail. "Merry Christmas" it said on one card, followed by "1914." Among the rest was a thick envelope from an unknown sender — probably some manuscript she was being asked to look through. Well, it could wait a few days.

By seven in the evening the family's little time of fellowship was already over. Each of them had really made an effort to play at celebrating Christmas for the sake of the other two, but without notable success. The invalid soon grew weary and retired. Mother followed him into his world. Filled with tenderness but also with a certain forlorn loneliness, Mi made her way up the stairs to the room she had occupied as a girl.

The thick letter lay there unopened on the desk from the day before. She unfastened the large envelope. It contained a number of light blue sheets on which was written a translation of the first canto of Dante's *Divine Comedy*. The unknown correspondent had also enclosed a long letter, which read as follows:

December 22, 1914

> The manuscript I am herewith sending you is an indication of what we have in common. Not the poem in and of itself, of course, . . . but the reality which lies behind it. For I have come into a world — the Dante-world we shall call it for the time being — which has excited my interest to a degree such as I had never imagined possible before. It is my dream someday to become an interpreter of that world and that way.
>
> It was about a year and a half ago that I first got the idea of translating Dante. Since that time the work has gone through many and varying changes. What I enclose is the final result. If each of the remaining cantos takes a year and a half, I will be very old indeed before it is all completed . . . . More and more one realizes that it would be presumptuous to think that this is something to make a big success of, as they say, for nothing makes one more humble. Yet one learns to handle treasures; one *learns* so much.

Now you are going to go along with me in my work, and when I have finished it we will both be very old, but we will have gone on a very wonderful journey which will be well worth the trouble.

What is of special interest to you in all this is the mysticism, most particularly the concept of purgatory. *Purgatorio* is the central piece of the trilogy. But it is the purification of the human soul, brought about by the cleansing influences of life. For the egoistically minded it easily becomes a comfortable cleaning-up place, merely a station on the road to the eternal celestial kingdom. And so it remains an *external* experience instead of something *internal*.

Freedom and *purity*, I realize now that, consciously or unconsciously, these have been the objects of my longing, and beyond these concepts is *the third*, which gives them color and background and is so great that one scarcely dares to give it a name.

Your — why not from the beginning — devoted friend,
Arnold Norlind.

So strange. And perhaps a shade too "sky-blue" to suit Mi. She tried to be critical of a point here and there, but really couldn't. There came a peculiar breath of fresh air from that letter, not from the words themselves, but from some place. The space around her brightened.

She had always walked quite alone in what the letter-writer had called the "Dante-world." Now on Christmas night itself she sat beside a companion in a great invisible church. She lingered there till it grew late, holding in her hand the letter that yesterday had been so disdained. Filled to the brim with a wondrous happiness, she at last retired, no less keenly aware that her old home had been carried into the valley of the shadow of death forever.

That evening she passed through a strange portal under a pointed arch so shaped that some bright wonder was always balanced against every dark suffering.

It was Mother who arranged a little excursion to Copenhagen together with one of Mi's good friends in Malmö. Mi needed to borrow some books from the university library in Lund and stopped there for several hours.

Should she look up her unknown friend? He had described his home as being on the edge of town with a view out over the countryside. He had mentioned the old housekeeper who took care of it.

She would need a signed authorization for the library: Why not run up to his place and get it from him?

Nevertheless, she felt a certain hesitation as she turned into his street. Just then there came by a long gangling figure, heading with light steps toward the tall house on Revingegatan. She could not catch a glimpse of his face, for he walked leaning forward carrying a large bundle of blue composition books under his arm. Beneath his hat she noticed a smallish nose with a pince-nez on a black string. There was no resemblance to a disembodied spirit, but instead a very real individual in a brown checkered suit.

A few moments later she bounded merrily up his front steps and rang the bell with a feeling that the dreamy quality surrounding the light blue pages had dissolved into something comical.

He was already sitting at his meal when she was shown in. But he rose to receive her with a simple naturalness. When she declined to share the meal, he calmly finished eating and looked at her with bright friendly eyes as they chatted about a book lying nearby. With a free and unrestrained enthusiasm, he told of a work he had just read. It was as if every formulation in it lay clearly in his mind, although he did not cite details.

It seemed to Mi as if he moved in a different realm of thought than other people. He spoke very clearly and simply and naturally, but to her he seemed enveloped in a peculiar atmosphere, as if he moved in another dimension that both brought him nearer and took him farther away from her own world. She imagined him sitting up in some tower, gazing at the stars, and that his look was just as bright and distant and wonderingly accepting when it turned toward her as when he directed it at Sirius or Cassiopoea. Having recently been so weighed down by her own and others' troubles, she felt as if she had been caught up in a current of air amazingly lighter than any in which she had lived up to that time.

She did not inquire why he had sent his translations to her. That seemed to be something just as simple and self-evident as when he wrote out the authorization for the library before she left, at the end of the twenty-minute call. He did not try to detain her.

Mi had a painfully clear idea of her own outward appearance. She normally paid little attention to matters of dress. But she happened to have on a ridiculously high narrow hat with a bouquet of artificial flowers just over her nose. It did not go at all well with her roundish face. The risk of an infatuation in "the dangerous years" was wholly out of the question on both sides. She laughed as she remembered how she had been trembling a half hour earlier.

They lived on separate planets in the universe. Just the same, she felt as old as Methuselah.

Mi often wondered why the "Dante-man" had chosen her for a correspondent. It was as if he were constantly pointing toward a space above — or more properly, within — themselves, and as if, in some fashion unknown to her, he had reached an unshakeable conviction that they had the same sort of road to travel. Sometimes several months would go by without any cantos reaching her.

Who was this untimely human being who had chosen to reach out to her along invisible paths of the spirit instead of seeking contact with her in the ordinary world? She was aware that he was a *docent* in geography. Someone had mentioned that he was an esthete and a humanist. But she could never bring herself to inquire about him of others. She left everything connected with him to live in a world of silence. Why she should do so, she really did not know.

Mi had long wanted to write a textbook, and that could be done just as well in her home town in Skåne. It became a simple necessity to spend the year 1915-1916 with Mother.

The fact of aging and the inevitability of death bore in upon Mi that wartime winter. Almost every morning she awoke in a state of mind which time and again found relief in prolonged paroxysms of weeping. In spite of all the joy that had upheld her, she felt as if she were somehow incapable of seeing light or of going further. Had she perhaps entered the "dark night of the soul" of which the mystics speak?

The gentle, old woman seemed to understand that things were not well with Mi. Each morning during this period, as if she had received a secret summons, she came to her weeping daughter. Cautiously she would open the door, put in her grey head, followed by her heavy form. And with indescribable tenderness, she took her seat on the edge of the bed and comforted Mi as if she'd been a shivering little child instead of a grown-up, experienced educator.

In spite of her mother's recognized intelligence and competence, Mi had often regarded her as fairly impulsive, optimistic and childish. Mi had come home to comfort and assist her widowed mother. But now things were reversed. It was she herself who became a little child that came crying to mother. How embarrassed she was!

When, during the day, she went strolling with an artist friend whom she'd known for many years, she felt nothing of her fatigue. Without the least effort she could bubble and be merry at such times. But each morning the same old ordeal began anew.

It seemed to Mi that her soul was dead and that what bore her name was an empty hollow shell. But then there at the side of her bed was Mother, awake and responsive again, now that one of her children needed her.

Mi's summers, and occasionally her Christmas vacations, were interwoven with the Dante cantos. Always they brought with them a friendly sense of security, even though for several years there were only scenes from the *Inferno* on the blue paper.

It became natural and self-evident that these pages should come, something like the change of the seasons. They belonged, and Mi would have missed them if they had stopped coming. But they evoked no special sensations when they came.

There was one long interruption of almost two years. The *Inferno* was nearly completed, however. The cantos reappeared, summer after summer, Christmas after Christmas. The travelers were already well into *Purgatorio*. But six years had now elapsed. The war was over, and one's thoughts were primarily occupied with the new world that must be built. Mi sent Arnold her Birgitta book — "With thanks for hell . . . . "

She sought sanctuary in a little mountain cottage. There would be so much peace up there, she thought. She did not feel alone there. She had a kind and thoughtful neighbor who had originally found this protected spot for her. Visitors from the village down below sometimes made their way up over the ridge. One day an older woman came, with her grandchild in a birchbark carrier on her back.

"I have an idea that you will understand what I'd like to tell you," she said. "You know the thing all the preachers talk so much about — well, that's what has happened in my own soul. It came to me after our Maria died, and I couldn't forgive God for taking her from us. We needed her at home there in the work and to cheer us up. Why should He carry off a 21-year-old from *our* house? When there are so many old and sick people He could just as well take home with Him? I couldn't work. I didn't *want* to, you know. It didn't seem worth the trouble even to set out food. Where the weeks went to, I don't know. It was a long while. But one day when I lay in the grass in despair, Christ came into my heart with joy and comfort. You know, I've gone to church a lot, but this was something I never could have dreamed of. For it was a *great* comfort that came into me. And you know, since then it has never gone away."

Did Mi understand! She herself had experienced this, and it had left its mark on her for all time. But she had allowed "Efficiency" to take precedence over listening. She felt deeply thankful for Ols-Mor's confidence. It came as a direct bidding to recover her sensitivity toward others, something that she had tended to neglect during her years of intensive work.

And now, as the Purgatory cantos rained down into her world more steadily than ever this summer, they had a fuller meaning than she had previously been able to find in them. Mi was unusually alone at this point and read but little. Despite eye trouble, it was a joyful aloneness, filled to overflowing with life.

Up there on the mountain, she devised a little childlike Sunday ritual for herself. In the morning she would climb to another meadow, much higher up, where there stood a lonely, vacant hut. From its doorstep, one could see much farther out over the blue ranges than from her own cottage. She would sit there in meditation for hours, as if enchanted. It seemed to her that the landscape of the soul was also being widened in some incomprehensible way.

On her way back, as she slowly and thoughtfully picked a handful of the red raspberries that grew by the path, there was a solemnity around her, almost as if she had received a sacrament.

During the seven years that had passed since Mi was in Lund, she had not met her Dante correspondent in the external world. But their exchange of letters had brought about something like a secure and durable friendship. They were both pilgrims, each on his own path, struggling up the Mount of Purgatory. Every now and then, they signaled each other from afar. Once in a while they also mentioned their own earlier experience in a general sort of way, usually with humor and a bit of self-mockery, rather than regret.

Taken in Hand by the Sun

The autumn after that beautiful mountain summer began for Mi a strange year of death. Three of her closest relatives succumbed after illnesses. And since Mi was on leave because of her eyes, it was natural that she should be on hand.

First she sat for weeks with her aged mother, who now longed eagerly for the end and each morning asked her to read hymns about the hereafter. And then came Christmas Eve. To everyone's amazement, the old lady rose from her bed, got herself dressed and put on her white shawl and lace cap, thinking this would make things more festive for her daughter. It reminded Mi of that Christmas when her father had been ill and the first Dante canto had come. Now there were only two of them. And her mother's very effort underscored not only love's happy power of defiance, but also the sorry limits of human decrepitude.

That Christmas Mi lived in a condition that may have resembled what the ancient mystics called *gelassenheit*. She really had no worries, but little initiative either. Their old family doctor did not prescribe any special efforts on her mother's behalf. So she accepted the days as they came, as if they were some kind of big heavy balls which she had to lift, or get help in lifting, gracefully.

Christmas morning, she awakened very early, filled with jubilation. All around her there sounded, as from a choir of many voices, the words, "Behold, I bring you tidings of great joy." The experience was all the more impressive since she was really not very musical. She did not think it was a recollection of a concert. The elation that streamed through her, something more than just the echo of a dream, was in sharp contrast to the outward reality. But she was glad of heart that morning, as she went in to wish her mother a Merry Christmas. Once more she perceived that underneath decrepitude and death, there flowed a wondrous current of light and joy. If one could only keep wide awake, so as to catch a glimpse of another daylight falling upon the hard and bitter things of existence.

Shortly after Christmas, word came that Mi's eldest sister, Fej, was suffering from an incurable disease. Her mother immediately dispatched Mi from her own presence to go to the aid of the stricken daughter. In the midst of her longing for death, Mother still had the invincibility of love. Mi was obliged to leave her and never saw her again.

The sister's inexorable disease had found a brave and cheerful soul to struggle with. She was a widow who had supported herself and her son, Rickard ("Putte"), by office work. Now she was physically transformed, but her old playfulness could not be concealed. Between bouts of pain she teased those around her into laughter. There was never any oppressiveness around her. She made wise arrangements for her son, whom she sent off to healthy and happy cousins. Brightly and simply and naturally she accepted both life and death. She held many pleasant coffee parties by her bedside. Friends who came to see her with long faces, ready to offer sympathy, left her with a cheerful smile. Sorrow had lost its sting.

It was indeed as the Dante friend wrote to Mi in a little letter after seeing the announcement of her mother's death in the newspaper: "Weigh love and sorrow against each other, and the darkness disappears. Oh, you know that well enough — this is just a reminder."

Mi's eyes were better. She began to feel eager for work. The long drawn-out waiting for death twice in a row had had a crippling effect that she knew she must overcome. It was not "six weeks at the most" for her sister, as the doctor had thought. She lived for exactly nine months after the unsuccessful operation.

Mi needed some books and went over to Lund. She remembered so well how she had gone there to borrow books many years earlier — then, too, at a time of sorrow. With a smile, she recalled the visit that time to the Dante translator. A couple of new cantos had come to her while she was staying with her sister.

She knew he had moved. At the new address, there were no staircases to climb. She entered the vestibule of a quaint, old, one-story house on a high stone foundation. An old-fashioned embroidered bell-cord hung beside the door with the calling card. But before Mi was able to touch the cord, the *docent* was opening the glass door. He had not seen her through the window, he said, but had had a distinct feeling that there was someone at the door.

Happily surprised, he led her into a room completely lined with books. There was a pair of handsome, high-backed, oak chairs, a large writing table, and, in the corner behind the door, a modest, narrow, iron bed.

This time they were so much more at ease with one another. He talked; she talked. Viewpoints and comparisons led them out toward wide horizons. It was as if they soared across worlds together. They understood each other as never before.

And how differently she saw him now than that first time! Beneath his light, wavy hair, his forehead was high and clear. The blue eyes, with that intense look she remembered from the earlier meeting, were now full of life and sympathy, and had a kind of bright gladness, as his narrow, delicate hands passed books to her across the table.

After all the watching and tension Mi had lived in beside the sick beds, the cool, serene, strongly radiant atmosphere around him seemed strangely healing and refreshing.

Earlier, in some ignorant way, Mi had felt herself superior. In this current of pure, refined goodness and genuine humility flowing toward her, her view changed. In the presence of this unique being, she felt like a monster of vanity and sullen selfishness. All that was heavy and hard was melted away, somehow, in this calm and happy air. She felt as if her inner being were transparently visible right through all that was petty and ugly in her.

A strange force took hold of her. Then the most mortifying thing of all occurred — she broke down in tears. She hastened away from him, angry at herself for having spoiled something that was so perfect.

Having had each other's company for so many years in the "Dante world," these two individuals had finally encountered one another in everyday reality. There began a new period when they met frequently.

More than once they walked in the Observatory Park, with its huge, old bird cherry tree that has since disappeared, but which he described with such enthusiasm. He had often walked there in springtime when the tree was in blossom, with some book in his pocket to read now and then as he walked; now, in September, it bore black berries as it rustled its upper branches mysteriously.

In Mi's situation it seemed natural to talk of death. The evening sky was already a glowing herb-garden of cloud-roses against a pale blue background. One star had appeared as they went along the road past the house where a prominent doctor had recently died without any previous illness.

For long months Mi had sat by sickbeds, where cancer or hardening of the arteries slowly but greedily ate their way through more and more of a beloved person's body.

"When the Litany speaks of protection against an evil, sudden death," she said, with feeling and conviction, "I would like to cry out from my whole being for a *good, sudden* death."

"You mean like *his* in there," said Arnold, nodding toward the doctor's house. "When Mother died, I felt only a strange kind of elevation. But perhaps I should admit that after the funeral, when I came into my classroom, something unexpected and surprising happened, as I sat there with all those good-hearted eyes upon me. A violent sobbing broke out, and I had to hide my face in my hands. I will never forget the pupils then, for it became very quiet in the class. No one laughed or moved at all."

They began to talk of their childhood notions of life and death and mentioned stories of journeys to heaven. "After all, what is the ascension?" he said, smiling as childhood memories came to mind. "Isn't it the way death and sorrow look when they are dipped in heaven, like the upside down image in a pool of water?"

There was so much of the child and the fairy tale in him. Perhaps it was the strict scholarly discipline which made his images resemble less the colored glass than its shimmering reflection on the wall. They lacked artistic form in colored material — they were simply like smiling air.

To everything that weighed Mi down that day he gave wings. He tossed it up into some radiant sphere, and when it came down again Mi hardly recognized it, so light had it become. And yet, he was so completely free of any hint of superiority. Was he someone who had finished his share of suffering, or what was it? There was so unbelievably much gladness in this gangling figure, walking the earth with such light feet. He had nearly been dancing under the bird cherry tree. Mi thought she had never met so weightless a being.

What would "people in town" have thought had they met these two middle-aged persons, who conversed so eagerly with such happy enthusiasm about everything between heaven and earth, the one clad in a mourning veil, which constantly went askew as she talked in strong argumentative tones, the other with an expressive voice now and then tinged with hoarseness.

Strangely enough, they never met anyone they knew on these walks. It was as if some benevolent genie had thrown over them a cape of invisibility to spare them from small-town gossip. They were a pair of lovers who could not tell what they loved most — heaven or earth or the Dante-world, or each other's deep understanding of things and thoughts — two who had walked astray and alone by themselves for so long a portion of their allotted span of years.

The "*docent*," who was now simply called Arnold, had grown up with animals and trees and flowers for playmates. True, Mi had hung on the garden gate of an evening, engrossed in the sunset . . . deaf to the call for supper or any other summons when the heavens were thrown open. She had had a pigeon and a little puppy to play with. But Arnold's friendship with plants and animals and the air was of a wholly different character, as she soon discovered. Just his way of looking at a flower or an insect had a quality of living it, of a *profound reverence in the presence of something other*, the like of which Mi had never seen in anyone else. When he spoke of animals, she thought he seemed more Indian than European.

He could recognize the different bird calls. And he clearly remembered how one dark evening he had first seen the world of the stars. Although he really did not describe things, she could sense how the reality was still living within him. It would not have required much more for him to make her see with her own eyes the images that filled his consciousness.

"Haven't you brought that approach to life with you into your scholarship?" Mi asked. "It seems as if your learning were not all separated off into some intellectual compartment, but as though you were personally acquainted with your countries and peoples and even climatic conditions. You spread some sort of atmosphere around every little straw and stone you look at!"

Arnold laughed. "If that is so, it is not reckoned as any scientific merit in my case. During all of my childhood I had so little need for words," he continued. "I thought people talked and quarreled much more than they needed to. I preferred to be out of doors. And my toys, few as they were, I would turn over to others. After all, I had the whole world out there for my playroom and my kingdom, and so I never felt any real urge to possess things. The kind of happiness that everyone could share was the kind for me. I thought I saw the whole world enclosed in a great gladness which hovered over it all."

"Weren't you ever in any fights?" Mi wondered.

"Well, I suppose I must have been," he thought. But he could only really remember *one*, and he avoided telling Mi about it then. One day, several years later, it came out.

The boys had built a snow fort and were going to defend it. They made hard snowballs that were iced under the pump, and then fought with these balls, hurling them at each other as they got the chance. Arnold had his piles of ammunition in good order, ready for the attack. One boy was hit so hard he bled. Arnold didn't want to hurt a playmate that badly, but neither did he want to quit the game. He took his position at the highest part of the wall, expecting to be peppered. One of the biggest boys on the other side rushed up towards him, but just as the combat was about to begin, the attacker stopped in his tracks, looked at Arnold in surprise and shouted, "What's the matter with you, Norlind?" and fled back down.

Mi thought of her own childhood play. She had been a tomboy who had had to prove that she was at least as good as any boy. She had certainly insisted upon her rights of possession. She and her brother "Bie," a couple of years older, had each claimed a piece of rope. They fought over it, each asserting his right. Mi refused to give in and held onto the rope for all she was worth. Her brother struck her determined hands so that they began to bleed. When her grasp became too deadened with pain, she was quick to take hold with her teeth. Bie swung the rope, and Mi held on stubbornly without letting go. After a hard struggle, her brother was afraid he would really hurt her and gave up. "And you know, I bragged about that victory — admittedly very shabby of me," she acknowledged.

"Now really, what faults do *you* have?" she asked laughingly.

"Gluttonous, willful and quick-tempered," came the immediate reply.

They remembered that afternoon in the Observatory Park and the later walk back to the station under the stars as "the childhood time."

But the first period of acquaintance also included what Mi called "the bad time" and "*the* time." "The bad time" happened in the library.

Arnold had sat down at the table where Mi had worked the day before.

"You've taken my table," said Mi quietly and mischievously as she walked past him.

For a time Mi was again engrossed in her work, but then, suddenly, he was standing in front of her in the reading room, almost empty now that it was the dinner hour.

He appeared greatly agitated. His face was pale grey, his clothes in disarray. He looked like a sick person struggling at any price to keep on his feet. His back was bent toward the light. His lips were nearly blue and his usually well-shaped mouth hung nervous and loose.

"I have always sat at this table," he declared, quivering with excitement.

Mi had long ago forgotten her little comment in passing. In horror she looked upon the being before her. She thought he was being dreadfully silly to make something of it. But most of all, she was so horrified at the way he had changed that she drew back as though from something strange and unpleasant. How starved and desperate and fierce he looked!

She seemed to be confronting a tense and lonely male whose shrill pettiness was in such radical contrast to the childlike being of a few days before. Mi regarded him with a distant look. It was like a bad dream. All the loveliness was gone, gone, she thought.

But when she returned that evening to her sick sister, now in her very last days, she had to tell herself that there was a great deal more of value in this world than the stimulating interchange with a good friend of the opposite sex.

The withered husk that lay there in the bed — a husk that made one weep to recall the warmhearted young woman of former days, with all her pleasant freshness and enchanting mischief — that husk was still able to communicate a wholesome loving concern for those nearest to her.

Her son was in the best of hands together with his cousins, and yet he would need a good long vacation after what was still to come. Perhaps he should go to stay with his aunt in England for a while, she thought.

"Do you know what I've been lying here thinking about?" she asked Mi. "If neither you nor Putte should happen to be with me just when I go, you mustn't feel badly about that, or think that it wouldn't be all right with me. My chest may begin to rasp a lot, and you might suffer from it more than I would and get worn out and exhausted to no purpose. After all, you have been here with me faithfully month after month. So remember, however it is at that moment, I'll be content."

Only two days later, when Mi happened to be away, the spark of life went out. The earthly remains, so incredibly thin and small, were soon carried to the mortuary. Mi gave up her room to relatives who had come from a distance and lay down in the evening in the place her sister had so recently left.

She scarcely expected to fall asleep, for that had been hard to do for some time now. But she must have drifted off almost immediately, and, when consciousness awoke in her the next morning, she seemed to be surrounded by a cloud of singing larks. It was so wonderful that she tried not to dispel it by opening her eyes.

"I wish you could have a little fun after these long dyings," her sister had said so merrily a few days before. The words rang in Mi's ears when finally she awoke, thoroughly rested and with the feeling that she had received a happy message from her sister.

Now she wanted to make things as bright as she could for Putte. She decided to go with him to England.

Whenever, during these eventful days, Mi's thoughts had turned occasionally to Arnold, he again seemed far away. But on her last trip to Lund to return her books before leaving for England, she met him quite unexpectedly on the library steps.

"Well, I must say goodbye now," she said. "It's off to England."

"Let me take care of the books; come out for a walk instead," he suggested. It was one of the very brightest of September days, and as she now looked at him, he was once again like himself, clear and calm. So again they walked together — "*the* time."

Mi told about her departed sister. And Arnold had a way of listening which made everything more significant than she herself had thought. They both felt so free in each other's presence.

This time she got a few small glimpses of his youth.

"Purity — that is such an awfully solemn word that it can't be used," he said. "Perhaps I might say that I have kept the space around my longing pure."

He had yearned intensely for a companion in life, but in vain. For a time he had actually been engaged, believing that his commitment alone would be enough to build a home on. But the relationship had not seemed genuine, somehow, and he had been impelled to break the engagement. As long as his former fiancee had remained single, he had felt he had no right to approach another woman with the thought of marriage.

Arnold became upset when he spoke of this. Mi wondered to herself if he might have lain awake thinking about it the night before "the bad time."

He had now reached an impasse in his career. He would not be able to continue his job after the appointment as a *docent* expired. Mi felt as if she, too, had come up against a blank wall in her work. For her too, a phase of existence had come to an end, although she did not say so to him.

She thought of them as two spirits out in space without any foothold on the earth, talking together about some former life. But with each other they recognized and understood all that far-off existence.

"I always have something basically happy here inside and only have to take it out," he said. "If one can only get his pail deep enough down into the spring, there is always joy there," he continued simply, without hesitation or unctuousness. It was as if he spoke of grass or trees that, as a matter of course, turn green when the season arrives.

He told about dreams and wanderings, especially of the glories of the ridge of Romele. When he was five, his older brothers had forgotten him there as they went eagerly chasing butterflies. Hour after hour he had trudged about among the trees that August evening. At last a tipsy butcher, who had strayed off the road returning from town, had taken the little boy under his protection. Now, in a way, he was again wandering in the twilight. But he was struggling ahead and soon all would be very bright.

What a child he really is, thought Mi.

"I've been living together with death so long," she said, after a moment of silence. "I think I haven't much life left. If I could, myself, die for the sake of someone, like Alcestis for her husband in the legend, then I'd certainly do it gladly, gladly," she declared maternally, almost old-fashionedly.

"That fellow who could let Alcestis give her life to prolong his own is for me the most obnoxious figure in all the world of Greek stories," said Arnold vigourously and indignantly. "Give one's life, yes. But to let others do it!"

Mi laughed. "It's funny, at any rate, the way we are walking here and have so many things in common. How should we describe our relationship? One of death, or of the life hereafter?"

"Why should everything have a name? It only makes us shy away from all that requires lofty words."

But now it was time to part.

"I believe that there is a Mightier One behind all this," said Arnold, looking into her eyes.

Mi hurried onto the station platform. And he walked home.

Neither of them knew that just at this time the woman who had once been so close to Arnold had entered a happy marriage.

Mi left Putte at his aunt and uncle's pleasant country home. In London she then spent most of her time in the British Museum, getting background for a book. She often took a break in the sculpture gallery. One rainy morning, she stood for a long while in front of the great column from the temple at Ephesus with its Alcestis motif. With a smile she remembered Arnold's comment about that "obnoxious fellow" who had allowed someone else to sacrifice her life for him.

She sat down to reflect upon her own past life. How would she sum it all up? She had been an admired little child who, at the age of three and quite without preparation, was displaced by a new baby sister. Long afterward, she was still reacting, physically and psychologically, to that dethronement. She had been a teen-age girl who was the "best in the class" and the ugliest in the family.

Later on, when an "admirer" did appear, she had fled precipitously, her heart in her throat. It was almost as when, at the age of five, she had stood holding her little sister by the hand. A lady had come up and tried to pat them, but Mi had cried out, "Don't you touch me, for if you do touch me, then I'll *screeeeam*!"

Once in her youth she had been in love. But the way led elsewhere. After that, she had felt absolutely certain that her fate was settled and that she would always walk alone through life.

At a very difficult time, the most wonderful thing of all had happened: the living spirit had broken through within her. There had been no outward intermediary, neither a person nor a book. But she had experienced an immense dateable liberation, Presence, Vastness, Inward Light.

The prophets and the New Testament had acquired a living content for her as never before. What had happened to her must have been something like what once happened in the soul of Paul — in proportion to *her* capacity to receive, of course. Now she could read his epistles with a new kind of understanding. She too had gone from death to Life.

All the talk in church and chapel had seemed so pale compared with what had been experienced, although sometimes she had recognized the same stirring behind the words. She had felt happy, bright, and free in a quiet way. That the goodness of God is the innermost secret of life was something she knew without help of quotations.

She had felt a need to encounter and understand others who, in different worlds, had received the same miracle. And that had led her to university studies, first in the general history of religion and then in the thought and history of Christianity. She had earned a degree in theology.

But, of course, degrees must be *used*! She had gotten a temporary appointment in a teachers' college and had soon been given permanent status. She had thrown herself enthusiastically into her work. Now she was going to teach about life as it really was.

Yet when it had all been converted into testable knowledge and practice teaching, it had come to resemble a collection of dried flowers. She had tried and tried to keep her teaching vital and at the same time to meet the requirements for objective knowledge and to give practical guidance in how to teach it.

The feeling that the spring of life itself was being mechanized had afflicted her like a genuine illness. She had tried to cure it with great doses of extra work in her free time, at the Workers' School and elsewhere.

But *other* people could manage "twenty-four hours of religion" a week without ruining themselves or the subject, she had told herself. What was so peculiar about *her*? And so finally she had decided to quit the job. But the wise and kindly principal had agreed only to let her take a year's leave, justified on the ground of her eye troubles.

And that leave had been used up sitting with the dying. Her life felt so impoverished, so exhausted.

She sat there and thought of Arnold. What was it that made her again feel Life — with a capital L — when she was with him or thinking of him? It was not his outward appearance that drew her, nor his intellectual gifts. No, it was a quality that surged up out of the unseen depths, an atmosphere of cleanness and goodness, an unconscious radiation of friendliness and healing light. Right through his shell she could perceive *the one who was greater than he*. Perhaps there was a similarity in their fates and their seeking, despite all that was so different.

Sitting there in front of the Ephesus column, she understood in a new way the meaning Arnold had assumed in her life. It was no storm of feelings that he brought with him, nor any sharply formed ideas that set her intellect in motion. Rather, it was like a vast horizon around a majestic mountain lake, where the winds and clouds were reflected in the transparent deep. And so much impish gaiety and childlikeness bubbled up when the waters were stirred.

What they shared existed on a plane different from anything she had known in her earlier life. Though "the dangerous age" did have an effect upon her, as it did upon others, that she would have to face for what it was. Yet she would not have been attracted by anything commonplace, only by something *extraordinary*.

As she sat there filled with reflections, she scribbled out this summation of her life in the notebook she had carried with her from the reading room. She called it:

THE ANGELS

The strange things from a strange world
forced themselves deep into helpless eyes.

The child's soul was filled with misplaced woe.
Shaking, it prayed to the darkness for death.

The trembling prayer found its way to the heart of God.
An answer He gave. — But death did not bring the message.
The angel Faith it was, who with consolation and light
found his way through mists of helpless anxiety.

The flame of the soul was lit. Life won meaning.
The world became the home of miracles.
The Divine rose and fell in clouds like flames,
sent trust into the quivering heart itself.

It came calmly to mirror the anxiety of others.
Pent-up forces were loosed in the joy of labor.
The lands of earth became patches of native soil,
that awaited the sowing of words and deeds.

II

Years hastened by in the gleam of the flame.
The Giver saw. His gifts must never grow old.
The soul's labor He let appear no more than dust.
Darkness and sorrow strewed ashes over the sown field.

The soul wandered on in the deepening twilight.
Beside it Death kept pace with his scythe in hand.
Cut down along the way were hearts and homes and thoughts.
Strength, wisdom and light fell victim to the blade.

And the soul sank down — was then the spark put out?
Its soil so barren and empty, its heart so wretched.
The voice of no living being came through the darkness.
What is sown midst ashes and stones comes to nought.

Mi had heard a living human voice responding to her own. There did exist a fellow being who understood her even in the darkness, and thus made it light. She felt sad that they had not met each other sooner. Why should she have to get so old and so spiritually poor before this new wonder came upon her?

And yet, it couldn't be denied. All that they had discovered in one another must be recognized as a *fact*, independent of the conventional or natural forms of association. But at this moment she would certainly have rather been like Alcestis. She thought she had so little life left to live.

And while she still lingered in the shadow of the previous year, her view of things spontaneously took this form:

III

Late and at long last the Giver sent the angel of Love.
It approached the soul. But not in sunlit clouds.
In high seriousness it came, with night and death behind it.
Sheer poverty it encountered when it came.
"Give your gifts!" the angel bid the soul.

All that the soul had claimed to own had disappeared.
Spark and youth and joy and labor —
All of it transformed, destroyed and gone.

"Give," said the angel again to the soul.

The soul sank down sobbing in the hidden depths.
Before the commanding angel it trembled and shook,
As once before like a helpless child.

"Why didn't you come sooner?" it cried in its agony.

But the angel of Love is the sternest of all.
No one can question it, only obey and give.

The soul bled under the weight of shameful poverty.
It owned nothing, was nothing.
Its whole being — was *nothing*.

"Give," said the angel to the soul.

A whining "No" was the response.

Then — all earth and sea and space
were icy cold, and there echoed back
a harsh, imperious, mocking "*No*?"

Speechless was the soul. In silence it gave —
its impotence, weakness, its grief,
all there was, And it lay as if dead,
the earthly shell broken.

But in space was heard the whirring
of the angel's wings.

Mi took the pages home with her. But she hid them in the bottom of her trunk . . . .

Mi traveled home from England by way of France. Arnold was on his way from Lund to Italy, having been given a grant to study some ancient charts drawn by mariners in the days of the great discoveries.

One thing was sure — they wanted to meet on the way. They did so in Berlin.

Mi knew nothing of Arnold's throat illness. And for him it seemed something quite unreal, especially since, on his doctor's assurance, he had a naive faith that Italy would make him completely well again. He had never known what physical illness was. And just now life was opening up in new directions for him.

Never had they had so much fun as in those two days together. They dressed their best for each other. The sun shone brightly on the late autumn frost in the morning. They were as exhilarated and frolicsomely happy as a couple of school children on a Sunday picnic. They went on endless walks, starting from the Tiergarten, near which lay the modest hospitz where they stayed . . . .

All the gaps in their knowledge of each other's past had to be filled in. They had been together so little in the external world. In many respects their separate ways had run parallel, and, when they met, each was at the end of one stage of life, had abandoned an old existence. It was like the passage in Dante's *Purgatorio* where there sat two spirits who had left one form of life, died away from it, and not yet found a firm foothold in the world, but who, just as they were, took infinite delight in finding someone who understood it all from the inside.

They were so amazingly, so immeasurably happy, these two grown children who had stolen away from their well-ordered spartan lives for a little adventure that no one else in the world had any knowledge of. And now and then they *had* to take each other by the hand. Mi's warm grip and Arnold's delicate narrow hand met one another. Her practical mind wondered about a little hard lump on his right palm. It was a callus he'd acquired at fourteen, when, overjoyed that his father had finally got his own parish, he had nearly worked himself to death for long hours in the neglected parsonage garden plot.

But otherwise they were not particularly demonstrative. It lay too far in. They caressed one another with atmospheres . . . .

Like a weightless being, Arnold positively danced over the heavy Berlin pavement. Only someone who has completely shed so many sorrows and troubles can understand such a free morning lightness of mind as was theirs during those days together.

And they came close to abandoning all their previous plans and setting off together for Italy like naughty children. How could two and a half days be enough for so much amazing delight? They were together beyond all time and attachments. Arnold had "not one foot of ground to stand on." The *docent* appointment had inexorably come to an end. And beyond Italy, where his health was to be restored, with the old sea charts as a practical excuse, literally lay the world's end, "Cap Finisterre." It was a matter of living in the moment and taking all it gave.

It felt so deeply secure to be together. No outward distances could seriously separate them any longer. From his childhood solitude, those long hours spent with the flowers, animals, sun and wind, he had come to live in what Mi wanted to call "elevation." But Arnold did not care for labels. Things simply *were* the way they were. For the little parsonage child, the sun had been the great monstrance that made the divine reliably and tangibly present and radiant.

> It is not so easy as one thinks
> To be intimate with the sun,

were words from one of his old rhymes.

A pair of mature, sensible people, a *docent* and a *lektor*! And even so, without any of their own doing, they had been taken in hand by the Sun. Some force as invisible as it was sure and cunning had led them, step by step, so near each other that loneliness, the life-long companion of each of them, was left feeling superfluous.

Their youth had flown. And now they saw that it had contained so unsuspectedly much in common, that the past itself became, as it were, a new organ with which to embrace one another. The same longing and intensity, combined with scholarly curiosity, similar experiences — and enough dissimilar ones, too — all of these gave to their togetherness a dawn-like gladness that seemed to have swept away all their sorrows.

No place was needed in the world of words for the miracle that they, beyond all doubt, belonged together. "Love" and "happiness" were not terms that it occurred to them to use.

One day an unexpected fate would make silence their regular guest. And therefore it was only gradually that the world that lay beyond for one would be wholly opened to the other.

Soon they would also be joined by another companion in their unity. In plain daylight, death would walk beside them like the unbidden twin brother of life. For almost seven years they would walk the narrow ridge between death and bygone days. Following the war one also lived on a narrow ridge between world epochs.

They kept aware of the great changes in the world around them. They looked upon it through the eyes of others and with their own eyes — eyes that, after years of study and living, sought to penetrate the surface of events, but also with much of the child's questioning wonder and hopefulness left over from all the unused youth that was no more.

Clouds of Apprehension

After Arnold and Mi's days in Berlin with the indescribable sense of at-homeness they brought to each other, Arnold traveled directly to Taormina. In what a hurry he was to *get well*! The "purgatory" he spoke of was the examination of his throat following his stay in Italy. Only if the results were positive would he feel clear for work and marriage. The whole idea of disease was foreign to him, and he had not brought the subject up with Mi during their happy days together. And so Mi did not understand the allusions to it in his letters. She thought it concerned only the change in his professional career after the expiration of his *docent* appointment.

At the hotels in Rome it was "*occupato*," and against the warnings of the doctor, he went on directly to Taormina, three days of continuous travel. "It seemed so easy," he explained. "The whole time I've been filled with this incomprehensible happiness . . . . "

For Christmas down there Mi sent him a children's book and a couple of "edifying verses." Two of them were as follows:

THE BRIDGE THAT ALWAYS REACHES

Only God and death saw my yearning wander.
And had I learned too early to long for someone
(who was not death and was not God)

while all my prayer was a dark dream-word into the dark,
how far astray I would have gone, hopelessly, sadly seeking
through all these seas and deserts, along so many paths,
that put a thousand miles between our longings.

And perhaps if I'd found you, but not God,
I would soon have found that it was not you
  my longing sought —

But since my longing first found God,
who gave me light to see you by, and all your spaciousness,
then its path becomes a mighty arch
surmounting all obstacles.
Out of the earth it rises as high as the sun.
Its way to you is God's heaven,
and it reaches everywhere and always there.

For God is love, the bridge for all beings
who have lost selfishness along some path of their longing.
Whenever God's Sun sends a ray into your space,
there I, far off, come with it to you in gladness.

MY MEAN DAY

What good is it to me that you hold me dear when I am "pretty"
because God's dear sunshine beams in my soul?

Nay, hold me dear when I'm the very ugliest of all
and only with help of your glance can find my way to God!

From Taormina Arnold wrote on December 29, 1921:

Is it terrible that I now write so soon again? But I couldn't help it, and besides, I had finished that difficult 25th canto in the *Purgatorio*, and then it is to wonderfully still here at my usual place. The sun shines in my face, though not too intensely, for it is still early in the forenoon. Right in front of me is the glittering wide highway that the sun throws across the sea. And the sea is so near that it is as though I only had to raise myself and stretch down to dip my fingers in it. It is a peaceful spot. The people talk seriously about "*la primavera.*" For us it is of course like summer.

And how good it would be to have you here on the bench beside me. You see, there is something I've been carrying inside for so long and that I clearly thought I had no right to say until I had gone *through the smelting process that awaits me.* But yesterday a certainty came over me that it was right to say it. To say, you understand, that for me you are *the only one.* I can't tell how and when this came over me. It has seeped slowly into me, and I have come more and more to long for you. More and more, and now I have to say it. With you I find just what one would like to call *home.*

And now it cannot really be wrong to say this, although no one can tell how the immediate future will take shape. You can call me egoistic, but I have such a longing to feel your hand by me during what is in store for me this spring and summer. It needn't be more than just knowing. Beyond that there will be the great new thing, that which will be so decidedly new for both of us. You see it is so very clear that our contribution together will be something much, much greater than what we could each achieve by ourselves.

Ah, my dearest Miglia, if it ever happened that you became really, really ugly, then you must know that just then I'll love you most of all.

But I hardly think you'll ever manage to get so ugly.

We will create — yes, we — an atmosphere that will be *nourishing* to breathe — for others as well. And let me say more. I'm also convinced that we will not be without the *Giver's* other gift, a child. Of course, *this* should have come earlier, but we probably were not mature enough. And when all is said and done, it is for eternity that we live, and *in* eternity.

As I sit here in the sun writing this, it has possibly helped me to find the courage to say it. And I feel so liberated now. It will be easy to go home. The sun's highway on the sea here below me has shifted off to the right and is broader and whiter than before. The sea is covered with fine ripples. Do you think I did wrong to say all this? You see, I believe that when something is of the nature that ours is, it doesn't make any difference one way or the other what we do. There is a strange sort of strength in what comes out of Eternity's chamber of light. And even if we should want to destroy it completely, what is indestructible cannot be destroyed.

You know, my throat didn't really like the strain, especially of that second night in the railway car.

Arnold

Just as Arnold posted this letter a cold blast struck him from Mi.

Before this new time of closeness, Arnold had sent in to the publisher his translation of the *Inferno*, together with a preface he had written when their relationship was quite different. Mi received the book at Christmas, and when she read his awkward words of gratitude to her, they seemed strange and impersonal. She wrote a mean little letter that was the first to reach him after his warm and devoted one. In spite of their experiences together, she did not suspect what a sensitive human being she was in communication with. Not until years afterward, when she reread the letters from Taormina, did it really dawn on her what she had done. "For all men kill the thing they love" — not only men, but women, too. And the tragedy is that it usually happens quite unconsciously.

In her letter she had asked him to bury all her poems. Unwilling to act without peace of mind, he had waited until he could do it in all serenity. He then went up to his Greek theater and buried the verses under an Indian figtree. For company they had daisies. By committing "The Angels" to memory, he saved *that* poem from obliteration.

Their relationship never experienced another such blow. Arnold accepted responsibility for it so generously that Mi did not realize until long afterward what harm she had done. And that was fortunate for both of them. For Mi was not serene. She would never have been able to forgive herself, and this would have allowed it to loom too large in their existence. And Arnold was verily not one to let others know or sense that they had caused him suffering.

Arnold to Mi:

Lund, April 9, 1922

No matter what happens in the world, *you* are the Only One. And it's been such an immense comfort for me to *know* that this belongs to eternity. Never for a single moment have I had to *question* it; the certainty has *lived* in me.

I realized that I still haven't said anything about my throat and so I must do it, though it isn't particularly pleasant. On July 1, 1920, I noticed a swollen gland in the left side of my neck, close to the vocal chords. My old friend, Sture Berggren, determined that there was a catarrhal swelling of a chronic sort at the back of the larynx and an inflammation of the so-called false vocal chords. During the course of the autumn he observed that the healing was progressing. It did not heal completely, however, before the place on the left side, the scar so to speak, became encapsulated. He was of the opinion that under favorable circumstances, like those I had in Italy, it would soon be healed altogether.

But this didn't happen. In Taormina it opened up again, but that lasted only a week. In Florence the weather was so raw and they did not provide any heat at that dreadful archive, even though there were arrangements for heating. And that is why my throat is still giving me trouble. It's only a matter now of getting this spot on the left side to heal or encapsulate. It is curious that all this should happen just as I am feeling such a high degree of eagerness for life.

Things are passing through a narrow gate for us both, Miglia. But then the path will broaden out again. We still don't understand the melody in what lies beyond. Oh, if only we could always remember that the more we quit thinking of self, the more power the Giver pours into us, through us, the power that sustains.

Your comrade in purgatory — with eyes fixed upon paradise.

Arnold to Mi:

Lund, April 30, 1922

One thing that really worries me is my throat. It is as though the evil was moving from the back part of the larynx to the front part, nearer to the vocal chords, it seems to me. Sometimes I can scarcely make any sound at all. A couple of times I have begun to wonder how it would be if I lost the power of speech altogether, how I'd have to forego "us," forego the "assignment" and —

In any case I stand in silence before the miracle: your world and my world, your space and my space, and then a great blue *our* world, with flowers and stars and trials and tasks for us both —

Arnold to Mi:

Lund, May 7, 1922

You see, ever since November I've known what it was that was wrong with my throat. According to Sture Berggren's diagnosis, it is tuberculosis. The x-rays showed that the lungs had actually been affected earlier, but had been healed.

My throat didn't really give trouble before I got back home. I'd been wondering if there wasn't a lesion there and I told Sture about it yesterday. He stuck his mirror down my throat and said curtly, "Yes, there's a lesion there." And so now it is to be cauterized. Early tomorrow morning I go into the hospital.

Now I think I've related everything. That this is just a short episode I haven't the slightest doubt. That word tuberculosis has such an awful sound. But then I learned that 60-80% of humanity has been infected, often without knowing it. And then the fact that my lungs are out of danger. Tuberculosis of the throat combined with tuberculosis of the lungs can seldom be cured, but a simple throat tuberculosis has a good chance of healing with the proper attention. And then, above all I feel so very alive, so filled with eagerness for life, so bursting with energy, that every thought of illness goes away by itself.

I've come beyond it, Miglia. I believe in our togetherness and long to see it deepened more and more. And the form it takes I don't want to decide. That is for the Giver to do, and it will not be long before the way will be clear. — Now I know that there is nothing in the past or the future that I can't come to you with.

Arnold to Mi (after the cauterization):

Lund, May 8, 1922

A few moments of pain that were nothing to speak of. The healing had really progressed normally in Italy and the whole right side was healed. Only on the left side, unfortunately, there appeared a lesion. "Tough luck," as he said, "for otherwise it would have been healed by now." I'm not to make a sound for five days. "The rest depends on you yourself," said Sture. And I'll not fail.

The letter about the throat operation reached Mi at Jakobsberg, where she was the guest of good friends at the folk high school. That same day she received a telegram of a very disturbing sort: a close relative had suddenly mysteriously disappeared. Mi did not feel she could unburden herself to anyone. She stuffed the telegram into her pocket and hastened out onto the road alone. She needed to gather her thoughts, to find stillness in the midst of all that had happened, all that gave pain and was so fateful for those nearest her.

She walked and walked without paying heed to time or direction. Then a singular thing happened. A big burly dog came and joined her. At first he ran along at her side, trying, as it were, to catch her glance. Then with touching persistence he began to lick her hands, now and then looking up into her face, as though he understood that she was suffering and wanted to sympathize. There was an unexpected help and comfort in it, for just then she would not have been able to endure the tenderest human approach in words or gestures. But this strange dog brought communication with the great spirit of Mercifulness, in a way she could never forget. It was no pure bred dog either, just a regular rough farm hound who could perceive her grief in a way she thought only the angels were capable of.

Arnold to Mi:

May 25, 1922

> In the evening a lot of anxious thoughts beset me. I seized upon some of the things Sture had said about the innermost part of the larynx, where his mirror couldn't reach. And then I thought that if that part were affected, it would be near the lung, and if it got there, all would probably be lost. And then there came such a terrible reproach that I had kept it all from you, and then I thought it would be best if I left you.
>
> And then I went into my very quietest chamber and *prayed*, something like this: Let me become a tool in Thy hands, let my actions express Thy will, let me be filled with Thy power in all my being, however frail it may be. But *if* the tool cannot serve to do Thy will, then break it asunder right away. It doesn't matter what it is, so long as there is some good to be done with it.
>
> And Miglia, when I've been in there with my questions, I always come out again with the surest certainty. There is such a sense of security in knowing that you, like me, lay everything in wiser and stronger hands. Let us once more see things brightly and be really glad. We belong together for eternity, and I cannot understand why we shouldn't experience "the short stretch" together, too.

That Pentecost Arnold and Mi spent with his sister Laura at her home not far from the old parsonage. They had some unbelievably merry, sunny days, when all the clouds of worry were dissolved by the great joy of being together. They made little excursions to visit the worlds of Arnold's childhood. Much remained as it had been. The tall, old, climbing trees, Arnold's perches in the wind, were still alive. He swung himself up, and Mi, who wasn't so bad a climber herself, soon sat up there beside him! They were as exhilarated as a couple of children on vacation, despite all the troubles they had been through, and, not least, those that still hung over them. They each had a remarkable capacity for living in the moment.

Right after Pentecost Arnold went up to Stockholm to talk about the new position at Birkagården's folk high school with Natanael Beskow. Without suspecting how close Arnold and Mi were to each other, he had been considering both of them for positions. And so it was decided that Arnold should take charge of the new second year course. Then there was the question of housing, which was quite hard to find in Stockholm. In Jakobsberg, however, there was a little cottage on a piece of woodland with a veranda on the south side and shielding evergreens behind — circumstances all very favorable for the respiratory organs.

Into that cottage they put their savings. Mi's share was really a gift she had received from a dear departed friend "for a book or a trip." And she thought the red cottage by the woods would be ideal for writing. By autumn Arnold's throat would be healed, so the doctor hoped, and they could move in.

During the summer Arnold and his sister would occupy the little hut in Dalarna that Mi usually had. There he would have the best circumstances for improving his throat. Mi would go to the west coast, bathe in the sea, and get some practice in household arts; especially some notion of cooking. It may seem strange that they were so confident about Arnold's health. However uneasy Mi had been, she became just as optimistic as Arnold when she met him and felt his bubbling vitality.

Together on the Narrow Ridge

Such a nutshell of a house they had, and such oceans of books that had to be crammed into it somehow! The number of books never seemed to end. They were floating in books — indoors, on the veranda, and in the stairway. Their possessions had been left for several weeks in a storehouse at the folk high school, ever since the day when the repairs to the cottage were supposed to be completed. They never seemed to get done. Arnold and Mi stayed as guests at the folk high school, but the time grew longer. And when the cottage was finally ready, everyone was right in the midst of the potato harvest, which was why there was no help to be had out there in the country. Arnold hauled books from the storehouse to the cottage in a handcart, urged on by the *rektor*, who believed in the virtues of physical labor.

In the confusion and in their eagerness to get into their own home, neither Mi nor Arnold really comprehended how absolutely foolhardy this exertion could be for a convalescent. Perhaps the only person who understood was a young girl, a relative of the *rektor*, and she certainly devoted all her energy to helping.

On the last day of September, when they were to be married in the local parish church, there still were heaps of boxes, empty and full, around the cottage. Arnold's broad, high bookcases from the university didn't fit in the low-ceilinged rooms. The bride, in her old cotton dress, was still unpacking an hour before they were to leave.

Their thoughtful friend and hostess at the folk high school jokingly made them leave off work and gave them a few sandwiches to take with them. It was high time they changed clothes and caught the train to the church in Järfälla. It was the same friend who rounded up a crew of helpers from Stockholm, most of them from Birkagården, to get things put away and straightened up while the bridal couple were away being married.

At the train they were each met by a sister who would be their witness, and so they had company to the old, grey stone church where the bell was ringing in the steeple.

A mild twilight reigned in the nave over the pews. But up at the altar, a pair of high, massive candles burned amidst flowers and greenery. The priest permitted them to speak the words of the marriage vows themselves without dictation as they stood beside one another in the stillness. Then, "officially" as man and wife, they accompanied their sisters to the station.

Their own wedding journey consisted of walking home together several kilometers in the transparently clear September evening. As they walked, the stars began to appear in the sky.

When they reached the cottage, they discovered that their friends had accomplished a miracle and then disappeared. The piles of boxes were hidden away and everything looked as orderly and finished as one could wish. Their thoughtful servant had set the table attractively, and so they ate their first meal alone at their own table with a great bouquet of deep red roses and the "world's largest" fruit bowl in which a giant pineapple with green leaves was surrounded with all sorts of fruit from many lands.

As they sat by the fire in their book room, it seemed as if they had always lived together there, so secure and homelike it felt for both of them. Arnold read poems in his expressive and resonant voice, among others his brother Ernst's lines:

> Ah, paradise and blessedness and spring,
> Resurrection and the scent of hyacinthes.
> Thy time of trial is past, the day moves on
> And the sun warms the winter of thy heart!

They *were* in paradise after all the rush. And they dreamed together of the future now beginning.

Mi would get the undisturbed time to write that she had been longing for. Arnold would go out among people to share his learning and spirit and the warm, human concern that was finally to come into its own. Oh, what castles in the air they built, these two who finally had one another. The Giver was felt to be so near to both. Life was wonderfully good, and the possibilities of happiness seemed boundless.

"And so it was evening, the first day."

The next morning he came in with a mighty cluster of grapes for her. There was a shimmer of light around his high shock of blond hair and the white shirt sleeves.

And as together they plucked the fresh grapes like a sacrament, he said, "I didn't dream that marriage could be so beautiful."

Several days later Arnold awoke with a very hoarse throat. Such an inconvenient time to get a cold, they thought. (How they could *honestly* make such a mild diagnosis after all that had happened is inconceivable, in retrospect.) So troublesome, just as the work at Birkagården was about to begin! In any case, it was fortunate that during October Arnold would be responsible only for a weekly evening study circle in Greek philosophy. By November, when the daytime classes began, everything would be all right again.

But it was not a cold.

Too late, Mi realized that Arnold's energetic labors in moving the books had brought irreversible consequences for his throat. The doctor tried not to frighten them. The word at first was that his throat must have a rest for a while.

How would it be with his work, this blessed task for which he had so longed and which would involve him out there with people? And what of the difficulties for Birkagården with the delay in initiating the new second-year course? The people there were helpful to them in every conceivable way. For the time being Mi would have to substitute for Arnold.

The months that followed were a strange time that brought trials and misfortunes of many kinds. Things seemed to collapse upon them as in the Book of Job.

Eventually the doctor confided to Mi that Arnold's condition was so serious that he could not be expected to live more than a year — perhaps a year and a half — with a throat like that, as well as the adjacent portions of his lungs, which were now also affected.

Arnold lost several thousand crowns on a loan he had guaranteed. It had been secured by a building which burned down after the owner had failed to renew the fire insurance. Arnold wrote at once to publishers who had earlier offered him assignments, but they now informed him that the work had been taken over by other writers.

They were left alone with poverty and impending death.

The little cottage was theirs, most of it at least. And for the coming year Mi could carry Arnold's work. But after that? If there were indeed to be anything "after that" . . . .

Each of them had often felt challenged by Francis and his way of poverty. Now it would be seen how much they were in earnest, these two who had loved the words of the *Fioretti*, "The brothers, like the birds, possess nothing in this world, but lay all in God's mighty hand."

Except for those closest to them, no one knew about their economic losses, and, for a while, no one knew the prognosis which Mi had received from the doctor and which she could not share with Arnold. After the first crippling shock, he recovered his courage and even his energy in an astonishing fashion.

During the quiet hours of dawn, he would lie gathering light for the whole of the coming day. He believed irrepressibly in health, kept on his feet and began writing newspaper articles about the draining of the Zuider Zee. The two of them rode the train in to the study circles at Birkagården. Arnold prepared the introductory lectures, Mi delivered them, and both participated in the subsequent discussion. A technique for mutual assistance was developed, and eventually it functioned remarkably well. The relationship with the study group was of the best, and the circle came out to visit them at their home.

Arnold could not tolerate self-pity. A Carthusian monk could not have waged his struggle more silently or with greater certainty of invisible allies. "How easy it is to be happy with you, in spite of everything," Mi could exclaim during their most difficult sieges.

Mi wondered at times how it would have been if they had lived in Stockholm as they had first planned, with all the bustle of the city about them and many other disturbing factors, far from the soil, the grass, and trees. Out here he had a protected environment, which Mi was careful to preserve. The illness, so inexorable, had the effect of making each day a day of grace, not to be spent in worry, but rather to be lifted up toward the light, not just to be suffered, but *to be lived* here and now as well as they possibly could.

Were these two people dwelling in an illusory dream castle? At the least, they inhabited a sunny isle, a coral reef in the ocean, where special laws applied, both those that governed poverty and disease, and those that were based on inexhaustible riches.

Possibly their greatest benefit came from the silence imposed upon them for the sake of his throat. It never created a wall between them. On the contrary, it released much "radiation" to which one would not have been sensitive if there had always been the highways of voice and speech to travel by.

After the worst blows, they sat on the two chairs in the back room under the skylight, where they often sat in silence together, and they thought about how best to order their existence. They had scarcely any debts, but in their critical situation, poised at the edge of a precipice, they were obliged to begin anew with quite empty hands. But work must not become a lifeless earning of money. Any task that really contributed to what they believed in ought to be accepted, even if it were poorly paid or not paid at all. Work that lacked any justification beyond pure and simple breadwinning they agreed resolutely to decline, even if it were highly paid. They must be fully free to help each other find inner clarity whenever either could see no way forward.

Arnold had a capacity to irradiate difficulties so that they did not get to be firmly rooted, ingrown anxieties. For Mi they at first had a way of popping out of their holes like jack-in-the-boxes, at least at night time. She spent hours worrying, not about the disease, which they continually *had* to reckon with, but, like the unbelievers, she asked, "What shall we eat and what shall we drink and wherewithal shall we be clothed?"

Early one summer morning after such a night, Mi went to the post office, as she always did. It was half an hour's walk through the woods and often brought great refreshment. On the way home she liked to seat herself on a rock ledge under a big friendly spruce and go through the mail. That morning she got back a magazine article she'd tried to get published. There was also the rejection of her application for a piece of work, and finally an appeal from someone she had earlier been able to help, but no longer could. She felt very depressed when she came back to their cottage to find Arnold sitting on the steps watching a wild rose. Beaming with enjoyment, he was looking at it as if the mere unfolding of it were a highly significant event.

With heavy footsteps Mi came through the white gate with her packet of mail. Arnold got up and lightly hastened toward her. He took the mail and mischievously laid it on the steps.

"Now we'll put all the worries there," he said. "And now you'll see how I'm going to shake them off." And he grabbed Mi by the shoulders and shook her coat. "You see, they're blowing away with the wind. It's out of the northwest today, so they're going back to Stockholm again."

"You're such a kid," Mi began.

"What's that? They're not gone yet? Then we'll have to shake a little more." And he looked so confident of success that at last Mi had to laugh heartily. With that she fell into another rhythm both in body and soul.

It was childish and comical. But it was something more than that, too. It was an absolutely genuine and inwardly radiating way of lifting Mi out of her slough of despondency.

Laughing loudly, they sat down on the steps with the pile of letters between them. As Mi now went through all the bad news with Arnold, things suddenly lost their bitterness. Together they hit upon something much better and wiser to do than what she had futilely attempted. Indeed, the messages in the mail became altogether pure profit in the end, however things turned out. Even for the requested help they were able to find a way that would surely lead to a good result.

The hardest time came during the first summer, up in Jämtland. They had been able to rent a summer cottage belonging to a beautifully situated farmstead. At that altitude, they thought, the air would be the very healthiest. All about them they had great mountains, lofty and glorious in their whiteness and the shifting play of sunlight.

Their hosts brought good food to the cottage — stewed cloudberries and strawberries with cream and all sorts of other things that Olersmor knew how to prepare. Her fresh and open countenance contained in the corners of her mouth a great deal of wry merriment that occasionally broke out in audible comment. Toward her guests she was extremely considerate and respectful.

Besides Arnold's sickness, which in this magnificent setting one *could* bear to mention, there was another nagging worry for them. At some point toward the end of the summer, their funds would inevitably run out. After the rent was all paid, they were not even sure how they were going to get home again. The new second-year course at the folk high school, in which Mi had substituted for Arnold, had been discontinued. They seemed to be up against a blank wall.

On one of the neighboring farms there lived a young couple. The sturdy wife now and then came to see their hosts, carrying with her a frail and waxen child, little Rune. Gradually they learned that the little fellow had tuberculosis, despite his obviously healthy parents. Passing by their farmhouse, one always saw a gable window open toward the north. Inside it lay the young husband's sister, stricken with a lung disease.

It seemed that "Aunty," before she became bedridden, had taken too great a delight in holding the child close to her. It must have been in this way that he had contracted the disease, for he had been born a healthy baby.

The aunt died and was buried during the time Arnold and Mi were there. Rune followed shortly after.

All of this was terribly depressing to Arnold. It was too dreadful to talk about. It was as if a killing forest came over his optimism. Mi never saw him so low as he was that summer in the mountains. In the mornings he lay there in the bed with the brilliant array of colors in the sky beyond the open window, yet his face seemed shrunken, narrow and bluish-white. He began to feel an obligation to isolate himself. His dream of having a child died.

But he insisted on getting up each morning to sit quietly or wander about in his old blue raincoat. He worked away at the *Purgatorio*, again and again struggling with the difficult canto about the origin of little children. Once Mi found him in blissful raptures over the triplet, "*Trasumanar significar per verba non poria*" about the inadequacy of words to express that which transcends human experience. Such moments were the exception that summer, rather than the rule. And since the injury to his gladness went too deep to talk about, and as the stigmatizing obligation to keep himself isolated became all the more pronounced, Mi also began to feel lonely up there amidst all the whiteness of the northern summer nights.

It was a night toward the end of July. There had been a great

Birgitta celebration down in Vadstena. Mi felt left out of such things as she lived in the company of anxiety and death and saw Arnold in need too profound to be communicated. She could not sleep. Everything was bright as day up there, and the questions were so persistent. How were they ever going to get home? How were all the other problems to be solved?

Long afterwards she could still see the narrow forest paths she walked that night. There grew great clumps of *Pyrola uniflora* beneath the fir trees, those tall, slender northland firs that stood upright like exclamation marks against the sky, but with nothing of maternal comfort about them. She did not notice the paths *then*, but they must have burned themselves into her retina. Later on she could recall it all at will with visual clarity, the ground pine and the lingon bushes in that all-revealing white melancholy summer brightness.

Her whole being emitted a wordless cry for help, for closeness. There was no way out at all as far as she could see. It seemed to her that they were lost in a *darkness that was white*, harder to endure than the black kind. It did not confront one like a wall, but came seeping in on every side.

Exhausted by the heartless brightness and whiteness all around her, she at last sank down on the forest floor. It was as if she were sinking down within herself, down into a bottomless deep where there was nothing to receive her. She had let go of everything. It was not the free courage of faith she had known earlier, but the extreme helplessness of the irresponsible infant, incapable of going farther.

After a time — whether it was hours or moments, she did not know — there came, like a blessed guest, a great security. Everything was clear. Somehow God was there, had come through the empty brightness as once before through the black darkness. An unspeakable joy came over her.

Calm and reassured, she pulled herself up. She even felt compelled to fluff up the moss and ground pine she had pressed down with her worries. She surprised herself when she laughed at that.

When she returned to the farm, the red glow of morning shone about her. Quietly she slipped in and opened Arnold's door a crack. He was lying wide awake and large-eyed as the celestial colors streamed in through the window beyond.

"Now you'll see that things work out all right," said Mi. And they took each other's hands.

The mail that day brought Mi the offer of several weeks of lecturing in Lapland and northern Sweden. The next day Arnold received a check from his brother for eleven hundred crowns in repayment of an old debt. Soon afterwards came a request that he write a book in his field.

And so they could cheerfully take the next steps along the way.

During Mi's tour in the north that autumn, delivering lectures evening after evening, she was met at every stop by a letter from Arnold. He was busy seeing through the press a little book for school use entitled *The Geographical Discoveries*. And he was already well into his research for another work on Rome in the later middle ages.

His letters told of everything he thought she might enjoy knowing and they enveloped her like a cloak of peace and security wherever she went, putting up in tourist homes or with families who provided hospitality for traveling lecturers.

"There is life and work here for me, too," he wrote. "You don't need to worry about me. You can leave me 'at peace in the hand of God's grace'. It is such fun to follow you hour by hour. Some other time I will be the captain out sailing the seas, and then it will be good to know not only that one has a mission to do, but that there is someone at home who is aware of it, carrying one along in thought and deed . . . . "

After that they could both stay home and work.

In the mornings they kept a workshop in the sunny dining room on the first floor. In yellow birchwood chairs at opposite ends of the oblong table they sat flanked by piles of books and papers. The atmosphere was undisturbed, as in a library. And when lunchtime came they had much to tell and confer about after the three hours of steady labor.

Arnold had a special knack of coming up with passages in books from his library for Mi to use as she prepared for her lectures. She did her writing on separate pieces of paper, while he used large yellow-brown manuscript books of quarto size. Neither of them had a typewriter. In an instant he could sharpen pencils or translate difficult Latin for her.

During those times when he was not even allowed to whisper,

they used little tablets for conversation. They devised a ridiculous sign language and during breaks acted out pantomines and charades. They had, of course, a lot of childishness to catch up on.

As time went on it became easier for them to earn a living. But both of them had been accustomed to steady and relatively ample incomes. Now everything was quite uncertain. There came times when it was not easy to get along without help, and yet they managed to do so.

Mi thought about the working principles they had drawn up in their chairs under the skylight. Several times Mi was strongly tempted to abandon those principles. One day she announced to Arnold, half in jest, but also half seriously, that from then on she intended to be unabashedly mercenary, at least for a while, and not give any more free lectures or speak for humanitarian reasons, but purely and solely for the money! Arnold appeared quite dubious about this startling proposal. And almost immediately there came two requests for Mi to speak, one from a teachers' association and another from a women's society. "I really don't care a whit about either of those organizations, Arnold," she announced with mock eagerness, "I just care about their money now."

"Well, we'll see," he commented.

The Friends of Elementary Education came first. Mi had two ten-crown notes in her little brown purse in her coat pocket, along with the return ticket. She hung the coat in the crowded vestibule before she went in for the lecture. She spoke on the Quakers, a subject that always moved her. Before her was an attentive audience, and she forgot all about money until afterwards, when the treasurer came with apologies for the meagerness of the fee — in all, twenty crowns. With fulsome compliments, he accompanied her to the vestibule and helped her with her coat. But the purse was not in the pocket. It had been stolen!

Mi was indignant. But she also saw the humor of the situation. Instead of the expected thirty crowns, her reward hardly balanced her loss. She guessed that Arnold would be amused at the result. They had a good laugh over her first venture in avarice.

Then came the women's society. They had once given Mi a really sizable fee.

"This time, at least, you'll see that I *can* be crass with success," she joked, as she set off.

It was a distinguished gathering, and Mi was intensely interested in her subject. After her lecture, the president made a pretty speech and presented Mi with a charming bouquet of expensive flowers, winter though it was.

"For such a lecture, there is no better way to express our gratitude," she said.

Mi went home with the extravagant bouquet, but without the expected fifty crowns. When she came upstairs to Arnold, she laid it before him on the blanket in all its glory. He sat up in bed with his brown sweater on and regarded it with a quizzical smile.

"Are you Pan, trying to conjure me out of my avarice?" she asked facetiously, but with tears in her eyes.

Arnold just stroked her hair and said, "You'll see that we can manage without having to do anything that isn't right for us."

Mi had thought that with her health and vigor, she would be the one to provide for their needs. But things developed according to rules of their own. Arnold wrote one book after another in the quiet assurance that if they worked and acted out of love, keeping inwardly free, then their lives would be in the best of hands.

When Mi was at home, surrounded by Arnold's atmosphere, she, too, was firmly convinced that they were following the rhythm of life itself and that nothing could be more authentic. But when she was in town and went into the shops and listened to the talk about how income should correspond to education and so forth, she had doubts about their right to live so differently and to be so unconcerned for their particularly uncertain future.

When she came home late and went to bed, she was tortured by worries about money and by anxiety over Arnold's illness, with death always standing there as the third member of their common life.

Yet not *once*, but on *every* such occasion she had a strange, but very real experience. Her thoughts must actually have wakened Arnold with their dark touch. Mi perceived physically how great lifting sweeps of helpful spiritual presence streamed in over her body and soul from the next room. If her anguish were too heavy or persistent to be removed, he would come in quietly and sit on the edge of the bed, until all the evil was dissolved and both of them could sleep calmly and soundly.

Their cottage had an especially good location. The great conifer forest came up close behind it. There were large windows on each side. In furs or his white linen jacket, depending on the season, Arnold sat out on the veranda and wrote or read in an easy chair.

Now and then, sometimes with Mi, he would stroll around the grounds among the oaks and the many birches. He could also take walks along the paths through the nearby woods. With a trained eye, he noted every peculiarity of plant or animal life. They each had a big oak tree outside their gable window. In summertime it almost seemed as if one sat up in a bird's nest amidst all the living greenery. But in winter the trees could appear like tridents with a gleaming catch of stars in their branches.

Arnold had to eat quite slowly, especially at breakfast. Since Mi finished first, they hit upon the idea of using this time for reading aloud. Many were the beloved books that they enjoyed together.

Arnold could not endure telephone calls or other inquiries about his health. Such intrusions were curtly dealt with, which was easier during their first years, when they had no telephone of their own. It became an unwritten law that they should do everything in their power to counter sickness and promote health, but not misuse either as a subject of conversation between themselves or with guests.

At regular intervals they drove into Stockholm by car to have light treatments of his esophagus or for cauterizing the lesion. Arnold did not like these frequent journeys for treatment. He put more faith in the sun and the veranda.

In spite of all his optimism — whether genuine or merely a device to keep their spirits up — their second autumn and winter were a difficult time for them. There were prolonged attacks of coughing and endless discharges of mucus. At times his throat was so congested that every breath meant torment for his vocal chords. Yet he insisted on working at his book. "*Nulla dies sine linea,*" he would say.

"Today I'm going to be mean and unpleasant," he might announce in the morning, but it would not be noticeable. During such periods, especially if Mi were away, he would write out his petulance to some friend. But at home he tried to be cheerful and reassuring, even when it was difficult.

When things were really bad, when he had a fever and was

confined to his bed from morning to night, then Mi would hear such remarks as, "I think it's hard to go on living like a good-for-nothing," or "My chest has to work like this just to stay alive." "Just now I love life more than ever, but when the body just feels like a burden, then one longs to get out of it." But this was a very unusual statement for one who was basically so bright and stable that he brought help and liberation to others.

His long and intense morning meditations, often beginning at dawn, were an inward preparation for the day and the task. Many an early hour Mi came in to him while the rosy light of morning shone into the room and he lay there as if transfigured, beaming with happiness. During such mornings, they shared bed and soul and joy.

To everyone, not only to Mi, it was evident that there was a glowing healthiness residing very very close to this sickness unto death.

At first Arnold could sometimes be beside himself in revolt against the obligation to whisper, especially when he met someone for the first time. It was hardest when he sat on the veranda and some wandering peddler came by. They either whispered as he did or shouted at him as though he were stone deaf, which both amused and pained him.

Soon he discovered that many people are happiest when they themselves are talking. A more attentive listener could scarcely be found. He inspired confidence by his obvious interest and the little words of response or explanation that he interjected here and there in the conversation. He had acquired an unusual sensitivity to what was happening within other people. They sensed this and told him things they would never have spoken of to someone else. Because of his intellectual training, he had less and less need to ask questions or seek explanations. He saw, he knew. Gradually something came to compensate for the lost voice. He could enable others to sense a certain atmosphere, to find the courage to be honest deep down inside. They, themselves, were often surprised at the strange and beautiful illumination that came round their own inner beings. This he did without having to talk.

Although few people in the area ever saw him, he came to have a strange attraction for those with troubles.

It was not that he was able to solve their problems. But he

could throw light upon them as he sat or lay there, fully listening. One would almost say that he *blew* on them — just as a mother would blow on a crying child's hurt and make it seem to go away.

Arnold and Mi had often seen a long, lean, broad-shouldered figure walking along the road. It seemed to them that he slowed down as he passed Lillstugan. Sometimes there was a kind of wildness in his look. If one greeted him, it seemed only to anger him.

One Christmas Eve, this stranger, whose name was Håkan, quite unexpectedly opened their door and came in. They invited him to sit down and share their meal.

"I can tell you," Håkan said, admonishingly, "that I wouldn't have had to be like this. It's all on account of the sickness. It's a shame to have to put up with this here lung disease. I caught it when I was twenty. There just is no justice here in this world!"

He went round and round on the same theme. It was as if all his grievances had finally been opened up and exposed to the sunlight. Tall and angry, he rose from the table.

"At least I'm healthier than you are, I can see that," he said, haughtily. Then he disappeared.

He was probably thirty years old. The neighbors said he was strange and retarded, and had too high an opinion of himself. He had been at a sanatorium but had been discharged as incurable. Now he lived in a cabin in the pine woods. It had been turned over to him and a couple of other men from the estate where he worked.

He was constantly walking about.

It was as if the red cottage he had to pass had blown a breath of air into his inward churning and annoyed him. He had apparently found out that a fellow victim of the disease lived there. Now, as it were, he had to assure himself that he was the healthier of the two. But there was a note of uncertainty in him also.

One evening, he suddenly stood in the entry way. Arnold was in bed, but Håkan insisted on being let into the upstairs room. Arnold permitted him to come up. He sat as far as possible from the bed, sullen and angry.

"What couldn't *I* have been, with my ability?" he shouted at Arnold, across the room. "By now I could have had a motor plow to drive with a cigar in my mouth. I could have had my own farm and people to work for me. Can there be any justice in life when *I have to be like this?*"

What were Arnold's thoughts at all this? No one knew.

But Håkan? As he continued his monologue, the very idea that someone might contradict him or even imagine that there was anything like justice in life agitated him so violently that he had to get up and leave.

"At least I'm on my feet, I am," he said, contemptuously, as he went. "My hands are strong and I can work my bit of ground. But what is *that*, compared to my ability? I should have had a motorplow and smoked a cigar."

He was enveloped in a stormy cloud of bitterness and pride, with an element of disguised sympathy mixed in.

A third time he made an approach. His fellow-sufferer was standing at the gate that day. Håkan took up a belligerent stance in front of it.

"I would have had a dog, and a motorplow and a cigar, I would — if there'd been any justice in this world. *But there isn't*," he flung out as he quickly walked off.

Usually Håkan was not talkative. But every time he passed by, it was as if he felt challenged by an unspoken argument for "justice" or at least for meaning in life — or for making one in spite of all.

The visits stopped. From then on, he took long and roundabout ways to avoid having to pass by Lillstugan on the regular road.

Was it that he didn't want to be confronted by any argument that threatened his own monopoly of injustice?

(Håkan's fellow-sufferer preceded him to new lands. The cottage no longer presents a silent argument against seeking daily nourishment from injustice. In it lives only a bereaved survivor who also is inclined to feed upon injustice, having no one to irradiate it or "blow" upon it.

"If things weren't so unjust, then — "

"Then maybe you would have had a tractor and gone around with a cigar in your mouth," whispered an impish voice out of the stillness.

She laughed. Someone did blow upon all the stored-up injustice. And she didn't need to ask where the puff came from . . . .)

And so they lived for two and a half years, with death at their side. Beyond the mutual joys of the moment, they heard a far-off, high-keyed melody. It rearranged the outlines, made the perspective vast and incomprehensible. All of everyday life was contained in a little nutshell of a boat which lay pulled up on the shore, but which at any time might be pushed out from land onto the mysterious ocean whose surf pounded so near.

This did not cast a superficial solemnity over their words and daily existence. Perhaps it simply placed life in a sharper relief against the background of death. There was always that duality — the shore now, and soon the ocean. One's gaze was not directed toward the world of solid ground. One accepted work and responsibility simply and straightforwardly, since each day could be the very last. It was a preparation under the aegis of life for the unknown that lay ahead.

Then that day came.

Suddenly, as if someone had called her, she went in to him in the silent dawn. He sat in the bed, white and motionless, as a red stream of blood flowed from his mouth. They exchanged glances. So, is this it?

He was laid carefully down on his back, just as white as the pillow, quiet and still as an inanimate thing.

She telephoned the doctor, who came with injections and prescriptions and a nurse and diagnostic possibilities.

But within the two of them, it was as if something dissolved the duality, that clear two-ness of life and death. Not that *one* of the elements predominated. At first, it was like a strange, thick vapor that enveloped them in a stifling cloud of ignorance. With the nurse there, the days and nights were long and heavy, without the exhilarating tenseness they had experienced earlier. It was like a fog seeping into one's throat and nostrils, always carrying the sharp taste of smoke.

The daily round of existence had to be maintained. Mi walked through the woods to the post office as usual. Mechanically she glanced at the letters. On the way back, she often sat on a stone in the woods. Mechanically she opened the packet of periodicals. When, in one of them, she found old *Jane Eyre* appearing in serialized form, she began to read it — she who had never in her life read a serial. It was like opening a little vent to let out the smoke, a way of escaping for a moment into a dream. She scornfully dismissed it as something primitive, but, in fact, it helped a little.

The days were so inhumanly long. It was as if she chewed the hours between her teeth, all the while with that peculiar irritatingly bitter taste of smoke in her throat.

Arnold was forbidden to move or to whisper. She was kept from him, also, by the professional competence of the nurse. It was as if they were secretly engaged and could only exchange understanding looks at a distance.

During the nights, she repeatedly dreamed of a dead child. It lay in its coffin. It got lost in the moving. It was expected but never delivered. And all the while, there was that thick vapor. One no longer knew what was sea and what was shore, life or death. All had been so mixed together in the lifeless calm that had replaced the earlier tension.

One night she clearly heard him cough, something that was both dangerous and forbidden. The nurse had fallen asleep, after having had a very trying time. Mi went to the head of his bed. They suddenly smiled at one another, a secret lovers' smile. It was as if all the mist vanished in the presence of this invincible closeness.

A deep sense of security had followed the long period of anguish. The duality of life and death disappeared and in its place there came a unity: love that needed, used, surmounted, permeated them *both*. They looked long at one another in the night, as through the window in the roof a faint starlight fell upon them. They experienced a communion in which they recognized a new element, a new relationship to life.

It is like the stalk of a flower. As it grows, it lifts new living tissues toward the sun. New light comes upon it, new strength enters into it, husks are split, buds burst — however one may describe what is taking place.

The nurse stirred. With a knowing smile they parted. Everything had "happened" in deepest silence. But how real it was!

The disease receded. There was definite progress toward further life, if not toward complete health. Their life took on a new unified perspective, completely independent of life and death, of bodily or spiritual communion. A healthy joy came over them, making all forms of life usable.

One could *plan* for this life without being bound to this world or limited by the prospect of death, rather in a sort of humor-filled readiness to accept life from everything, every occurrence and situation. The beached boat waiting to shove off on to the sea no longer provided a satisfactory image for their existence.

They were both well along the way beyond all of it, two migratory birds that could spread their wings or simply be at rest, feeling at home beyond events.

As never before, their neighbors' friendliness was poured out upon them that Christmas. From his woodlot their friend Larsson brought two fine juniper bushes and planted them by their door. A shy young man came to deliver a Christmas tree as a present from his family. Little girls came with flowers and evergreen boughs. It was as if they had all shared the tense life-and-death struggle and wanted to show their happiness.

Arnold and Mi seemed to be beginning a new sort of daily life when at last Arnold was up and around again. He had been like a "guest and sojourner" on this earth. But he made the most earnest efforts to involve himself in the here and now of life.

"If only both of us," Mi once exclaimed, "could leave all this at the same moment." She remembered his bright response: "There is no running away that can liberate, not in *any* heaven. There is only *right on through*. And then heaven is there, in you and with you . . . . "

Now and then Mi, herself, thought how Arnold's potentialities, all his vital fund of learning, were not being utilized by society, how all this richness of life was being confined to such an extremely narrow world, within this wasted frame, in this little cottage, with its few poor neighbors, so cut off from intellectual contact.

The question of work again became urgent for Mi. If, in spite of Arnold's chronic illness, they could start life anew, they might be able to make some contribution to the large world they were part of, where the postwar optimism was already yielding to the forces that were preparing new wars. There were things that called them, though without outward pressure.

Faithful to old patterns, for several years they conducted study circles. They wanted to share what they had, even though the part of the parish where Lillstugan was located lay at quite a distance from the community around the railway station, as well as from the church village. Now and then the housewives of the neighborhood came together for an afternoon of work, combined with reading aloud. There was no one else to gather them, and they enjoyed it.

Once a week there was a study circle in English. It was free of charge, and the five members, very different though they were, were very regular in attending. They consisted of a young gardener and his assistant, a sailor looking for work, an intelligent schoolboy, and a refined and musically gifted young metal worker. The last two exhibited great diligence and made remarkable progress.

Although his achievements were minimal, it was the gardener's helper who never missed a time. They saw him every day at his work, dirty and dishevelled. But when it was time for the study circle, he was neat and clean beyond recognition. His hair was erect from all the pomade it had been given in honor of the circle, and on his clean grey sweater there shined a red pin. Almost all of them wore some sort of club badge. The metal worker belonged to a Christian youth organization.

It was really Mi who conducted the circle. But Arnold often came down to greet them. Or they went up to see him. Especially with the gardener's helper, he developed a close rapport. One day when Mi was away, Andersson had come and complained about his difficulties to Arnold. For several years after he left the area, he sent Arnold the choicest and most expensive Christmas cards he could find. Communist though he was, his greetings were always adorned with angels and church bells. Whenever he got in a pinch, he would write to Arnold, confident that he had every possibility of helping him.

Several factors influenced their decision to leave Jakobsberg. For one thing, they greatly cherished the slender hope that they could both use their energies as though they were healthy people.

Arnold's throat was by no means ready for normal activities. But he thought he could manage his research in the library. He could walk greater distances than he had been able to do for several years, and he was showing up on foot as far away as the post office and the railway station.

Mi had begun work on a book about the psychology of mysticism. She had delivered two long series of lectures on the subject for teachers in Stockholm. But she had had to lay the manuscript aside. It seemed easier to take up some topic that was completely new to her. And thus she began her study of the seventeenth century Quaker James Nayler, a figure in whom the noblest and purest aspirations were brought to shame by an appalling tragedy, yet in whom the irradiating power of reconciliation ultimately turned darkness into light.

Mi was altogether captivated by this work. Yet despite the shipments of books and copies of manuscripts she was able to have sent from England, it was going to be necessary for her to go there to examine the material directly. Arnold and she agreed that she would try to spend a fortnight in London, once the moving was behind them.

She applied for and received a grant from the Lars Hierta Foundation, as well as help from some other sources. But first it would be necessary to get money to pay for the moving, which was scheduled for November. To do that she set off on a lecture tour.

At every stop she found a letter from home. In one of them Arnold spoke of,

> the indescribable benefit of feeling more like a human being again. To be able to walk erect, to hold your head high, to stand up and feel the ground under your feet. You don't realize how a long illness can make you feel inferior. And then to feel human again — that *is* a restoration. Not to be the spectre's slave any more, as William Blake says. In body I feel fine. We both know how wonderfully our angels have led us and helped us, the visible angels and the invisible ones — and they both must be related somehow. One looks at these six years and our home here in Lillstugan with boundless gratitude. Many thanks, little cottage!
>
> There are stars here tonight. Yes, yes, we are indeed close to the stars. *The Bridge of San Luis* is surely a book we ought to read. I send star-greetings. Good night.

And so they dared to hope for health.

"The farther we go up the Mount of Purgatory, the easier it gets," Arnold used to say. And it was true. But the "light air" did not mean bodily health.

The remaining steps of the ascent were to be perhaps the heaviest ones.

An important element in their existence had been the kindly and intelligent servant who had seen them through the first difficult years. But Anna was slight and frail. Once when she was suffering from a bad cold, she became very disturbed by the thought that she was infected with tuberculosis. One day while Mi was away she revealed her anxiety to Arnold.

"Now we will have to let her go, even if she doesn't want to," he said. "We can't be responsible for her having worries like that. But before anything else we must see that she gets examined by a doctor."

To their immense relief there proved to be nothing wrong with Anna's lungs. They would have to separate, nonetheless.

They happened to remember an attractive woman up in Jämtland who, a couple of years before, had suggested her only daughter as a household helper. So they wrote to Karin asking if she could come to work for them starting the first of October, provided the doctor examined her lungs and saw no risk in her coming.

Karin arrived, ever so cheerful and willing and trusting. She was especially pleased at the thought that in November they would be moving into Stockholm for the winter. For the first three weeks, everything went smoothly.

Then, all at once, Karin became silent and reserved. One morning, she appeared flushed from crying, her eyes fearful. The evening before, she had been to visit a neighbor. Up there in Jämtland, said Karin, they hadn't understood that it was the dreadful contagious disease. When they had required that she have her lungs examined, it was supposed that her employers were concerned for themselves. But now she had learned from the neighbors the awful truth.

So Karin had to go.

It was one thing to try to protect an anxious soul; it was quite another to find oneself shunned like the plague.

Mi tried to soften the blow when Arnold had to be told. For a while they could get along with temporary help. Good friends would assist them with the moving, and in a couple of months they hoped they could find a suitable person who would not be afraid.

But once again they had stumbled upon the irrational.

Two Men Talk of Death

Arnold lay there so quietly that Sunday evening. It was their last night in Lillstugan and the world of Jakobsberg.

It began to get dark in the upstairs room, but the heavy red geraniums still caught a few splashes of sunlight by the window. One flickering beam found its way across to the bed in the corner.

Heavy steps sounded from down on the porch. There was the clatter of the lid being removed from the large milk can. It was the farmer himself. He had been a widower for several months, and the hired girl he had taken on had soon left.

Presently he stood inside the kitchen door. The strong smell of stable and earth enveloped him, as if he had just sprouted up out of the ground, bringing with him the ghosts of all the cows and pigs he had cared for in his life. He had never had children. Perhaps that was why he loved his animals as if they were his own flesh and blood.

"When is the professor leaving?" he asked bluntly as Mi poured the milk into a large brown crock.

"We go tomorrow," was the reply.

"Then I'll go up and say goodbye to him now tonight," said Larsson in a decisive manner, implying that he did not intend to be prevented.

He slipped off his wooden shoes and in stockinged feet climbed to the upper room. He knew well enough that his knock would bring no loud "Come in," but he also knew that sickness had taught the one he was visiting the art of conversing with people without using his voice.

Lying on the bed, Arnold nodded and smiled. They shook hands. The two hands were very different in size, shape and color. Mi slipped quietly into the next room.

Larsson sat down on the chair by the desk and turned toward the bed. He sat silent a moment. Then he blurted out, "When you're dead, you're dead. That's all there is to it. When you're dead, you're dead."

But after a minute or so, it seemed to him that he had said something out of place. After all, the sick man himself knew something of death — had lived with it a couple of years. So he changed the subject to their great common interest, their love for animals.

"Animals die so easy," he said. "It happens all at once. They don't have a lot of agony — no pain to it."

Silence fell again. But a weightless silence.

It became more and more like a great bright space, where it was easier for Larsson to talk.

"My woman, she died easy, too," he said softly. "We went to bed in the evening as usual. And even though it was still winter, we lay there and talked about what we would plant next spring. We agreed on it. But when I woke up in the morning, she lay there dead in the bed beside me. There on the stove stood my boots, which she'd greased the day before. There lay my mittens that she'd sat up and darned in the evening. But no matter how much I called her, she was dead. But there lay the mittens. And the boots — there they stood."

After a short pause he spoke again. "But she died so easy. She was so kind. Don't think I'll die that easy." There was a soft sigh. But again came the refrain, "Yeah, when you're dead, you're dead. That's all there is to it." This time there was something more like an anxious question behind the firm assertion.

It began to be dark. A slight breeze rustled in the oak outside. The mild fall had spared most of its leaves. The geraniums had lost their color and become a dark shadow against the space of the window.

"And yet it's a funny thing," Larsson continued, "the longer I'm alone, the more it seems as if Karna comes to help me."

One could scarcely distinguish the face in the bed, so dark it had become up there in the bookroom. Larsson went on as if he were by himself, but as if out of the silence there came something that strengthened, something that helped him find the power to express all he had kept silent in his pain and confusion. At last he ventured on.

"Now just the other day. Of course, I had to hire help with the potatoes, there wasn't any other way, when I didn't have Karna. It was Hagman, and he had to have regular food. So I bought things for a stew. But how was I to fix it?"

Larsson now leaned forward secretively toward the bed and spoke more softly, as in the deepest confidence. "Then I seemed to hear Karna's voice say, 'Take the allspice, Nils, and the bay leaves.' But I'd no idea where she kept the spices, I'd not seen them since she went away. It was as if a hand led mine straight to the inside corner on the left side of the chimney cupboard — and there were her jars and leaves.

"I felt so happy in a funny way. I tossed the stuff into the kettle. And so we had dinner. Can you guess what Hagman said? 'Yeah,' he said, 'This is good stew, Larsson. Darn if it doesn't taste like a woman cooked it.' That's what he said, really."

Again it was quiet for a while. A star appeared outside the window, a small one, with a feeble gleam.

At last Larsson shook himself loose from his thoughts. No doubt it was the sounds of the animals that called him. Once more the smell of the stable became noticeable through the half-open window by the desk.

"Yep, when you're dead, you're dead," said Larsson for the third time, quite absent-mindedly, just as he rose to go.

"*Think so?*" whispered Arnold, mischievously, and looked warmly at Larsson as they shook hands. Larsson gave a start. It was as if he became aware that he himself had contradicted the import of those words and had repeated them like a worn-out phrase, like the chaff on the barn floor when the grain has been threshed out.

There was something clear and peaceful about him when he came down the stairs again in his stockinged feet.

But the silence that still filled the room was permeated with light and wonder. Out of the quiet came a *smile*. Who smiled? At what? At the stew — or at what we human beings call death?

Moving and Afterward

With the help of Birkagården, they found a sunny, three-room apartment with a shower. It was close to Karlberg Park and Solna Woods. In the same building lived many dear friends, which was reassuring to Mi as the time for her departure for London drew near. Their friends found a temporary servant for them right away. Eventually things would go well when that competent woman from Västmanland came to take charge of the household. Indeed, one could not ask for a better arrangement.

The moving went smoothly thanks to many helping friends, in addition to the professionals. Arnold's "proper" tall bookcases from Lund, stretching from the floor to the ceiling, could again be put to use. Although the books were only placed in a hit-or-miss order to keep them from being all over the floor, they would not be a problem, and Arnold had promised to have as little to do with them as possible for the time being.

One of their closest friends stayed in Mi's room and saw to things during the two weeks Mi was away in England.

Mi crossed the North Sea in a dreadful storm that delayed her arrival by 24 hours and, in contrast to all previous experience, made her really seasick. She stayed at the home of a university-trained English Quaker, Mrs. Maynard, who over the years was to become her dear friend. At the Friends' House Library she got excellent help in using the archives. And, best of all, each morning, as she came in, she saw from a distance that never failing white oblong on her library table — a letter from Arnold.

She kept each letter close to her as she worked at full speed. At closing time, she was permitted to take precious materials out of the library so she could get in a few more hours of work.

But no matter how Arnold tried to encourage her with accounts of everyday events, Mi noticed a melancholy note between the lines.

Oh, if Mi could only have had a few more hours in the day! Or if she had had the energy to be able to work all night! But on the morning of the ninth day, she felt strongly that she had to go home, and nothing in the world could hold her back. She selected manuscripts of which copies were to be made and sent to Sweden. She was permitted to take with her some valuable volumes from the library.

So Mi arrived home again, quite weary and worn out after the heaviest workload she had ever imposed upon herself.

As soon as she laid eyes on Arnold, she knew that he had taken a turn for the worse. At the moment, he was delighted with a translation of Euripides' *Trojan Women*, which he was making for the actress Gerda Lundequist. But when he proudly announced, "I've got all the bookcases ready for your homecoming," Mi was horrified and thought all sorts of dirty words about books and bookcases.

How pale he was, and how loud his breathing!

"Oh, you'll see, it will pass over right away. Soon I'll be really healthy," he said.

Shortly before moving, they had received Thorton Wilder's book *The Bridge of San Luis Rey* from a friend in America. That book — about how death comes to each of the characters at just the right moment — was to be the last book they would read together.

By the end of January, Mi's manuscript was finally ready for the publisher. Arnold had finished the *Trojan Women*. Now they were able to have a really good rest. But Arnold was not at all well, and Mi was feeling ill and feverish. Nor could she relax completely, so long as they had not found a permanent household helper.

The first Sunday in February, they were visited by a friend whose husband lay seriously ill at a sanatorium in Norway. She could not leave her small children just then to go to him as she had wanted. She sat a while beside the bed where Arnold lay so white and motionless, at the very moment, they learned later, when her own husband was breathing his last off there in the mountain sanatorium. The broad band of sunlight from the wide window fell upon the bed and the two quiet people there, Arnold and the guest. It was so wonderfully beautiful, that band of sunlight. To Mi, sitting across the room, it seemed that they were surrounded by a strange far-away light that belonged to other worlds.

Arnold was now too sick to leave his bed. Was it an intestinal influenza or —? Mi herself was running a fever. I've got to go up to see Dagny Thorwall, she thought, and find out if our maid can't come a little sooner than she promised. The stairs seemed endless that day as she stumbled up them. The answer she got was the opposite of what she had been hoping.

The offer had been cancelled. Their hoped-for servant had a sister who worked for a family in Stockholm. The sister's employer had told her emphatically that if a maid of *hers* associated with someone who worked for a tubercular patient, she would be dismissed at once!

Mi was stunned. She could *not* let Arnold hear about *this*. She would have to handle it all by herself. But how? She almost tripped as she pushed by Arnold on her way into her bedroom.

Quite mechanically she took her temperature, which she had neglected to do earlier. It was 38.9 (104.5 Fahrenheit). She collapsed on top of the bed. Both of them were sick, and under such circumstances Arnold would have to have a nurse.

Mi lay shaking with chills and fever all that evening and through the night. Sometimes she wandered out into the hall. But the nurse, a kind and warmhearted young woman, could take better care of Arnold than she could.

She lay down again. There was nothing else she could do. All at once things had come to an end for her. Was it the fever that haunted and tormented her? Or was it some sinister spirit? It was like the laughter of some cosmic being that had come to mock all that the two of them had believed in and sought to accomplish. Previously, whenever they had found themselves up against an impenetrable wall, the wall had always eventually given way and they had proceeded happily onward. But now it seemed that she couldn't even desire anything anymore, as if they stood at the end of everything.

A thousand rebellious "whys" surged up within her. It was the first and only time in her life that she understood how people could believe in a metaphysical devil. Her need stretched all the way to the underworld of the soul, "in the power of death and Satan." Nothing she had ever experienced — or read about — had been like this. It was as if the arrows of evil had shattered their whole world.

Then right through the doors and walls came a warm soft wind sweeping in over her. Oh, she recognized it! Well did she know where it came from.

If only she might tell him the latest crushing news about their help, so that he would understand why she had rushed through the room without saying anything. Perhaps in some way he already did know about it, for he could pick up beams and vibrations, the motions of the spirit, without any words.

She managed to grope her way to the light switch, and took up the English Bible lying nearby. Over and over again she read a few verses — those final ones in the eighth chapter of the Epistle to the Romans — that had burst forth from experience that is really audible only to souls grappling at the very deepest level. She *heard* the meaning of the words. Tangibly and simultaneously she also felt helping thoughts coming from Arnold right through the closed doors.

Her fever subsided noticeably. Very early, she got up and dressed. She was clear and calm that morning as she went through the hall and in to Arnold.

As soon as she saw him, she understood that he was about to *go*.

Sitting there at the edge of the bed, she passed beyond all thought of self or of fever.

Arnold fought for breath the whole forenoon. His eyes seemed so far away . . . . In the room outside sat some of their closest friends at Birkagården. Suddenly and quite unexpectedly, his brother Ernst Norlind looked in for a moment. Arnold gave him a smile of recognition.

By four o'clock, the lonely agony was over, and for an hour Arnold came back to Mi completely, with his eyes, with both hands, with his whole, great, rich, loving being. She felt as if he understood everything. He literally lifted and carried her.

"Now you're the captain of our boat," she said, smiling through her tears, as she recalled an old jest of theirs. Arnold smiled back. They were one.

When finally he lifted his head and chest and drew his last breath, he wore an exquisite look of marveling blessedness and deepest humility. "When saw we thee, Lord?" It rose into something so wondrous that such an other-worldly smile can only be intimated here on earth.

He wasn't gone at all.

Every time Mi began to wonder "if we had done this or done that," or her memory reverted to that terrible night he was present within her and simply swept it all away. For months afterward, she lived in a strange state of inward radiance.

Her soul was wide open. There was no grief, as she remained in the afterglow of that last powerful wave of love, of that last smile and that unreproducible perception of a sunlight that shone from within. It was not the far away lumination that had enveloped the bed the previous Sunday. No, it was warm, alive and buoyant.

Sunday's child had moved on — on a Sunday. From the many letters, greetings and conversations about him, Mi could have assembled a little collection of miraculous legends, as in medieval times.

Little things happened to her — but words are not adequate to capture their meaning.

Mi had been lifted up on the crest of a mighty wave, from which she gained a new view of heaven and sea and earth. It felt as though she were inside the element of Life itself. Death did not exist.

The first time she went out on the street again, there suddenly welled up out of her unconscious the naive thought, "Now Arnold and I can always go out walking together."

The friend who had given them the summer in Jämtland offered Mi the opportunity to spend the weeks following the funeral in the Alps. Arnold was continually with her there as though on a mount of transfiguration. They shared a secret, common joy. Now no beauty seemed to pass unappreciated. She could look upon the things of Nature, great and small, in *his* way, with more empathy than ever. Down here, she wandered about in an Elysium of spring flowers. And there were always two who saw them.

On the anniversary of Arnold's passing, February 17th, she went out to the empty cottage in Jakobsberg. A clump of Christmas roses she had never seen before was blooming bright against the snow. And up in Arnold's bookroom, where the head of his bed had stood, sat a moth. It was no dream-butterfly, just a common, big, red and brown moth.

Mi did not escape grief and the feeling of loss. They came later. On journeys and voyages, in America and Sweden, there burst forth short monologues that belonged to the Arnold-world.

I become so hard when you are gone.
All the walls I've built for self-defense,
that you concealed —
just as the sun
and sometimes the mist
disembody heavy things,
making them airy, so they exist
in contour, lines only,
but no longer hard and heavy things.

And you who in life overcame
coarse-mindedness, ambition,
a distant coldness toward all life,
you who tried to keep your dwelling
pure as a temple of heaven,
you broke asunder your dwelling!

But all that goodness and that purity
which could not be confined to real estate,
which in this dwelling felt hemmed in,
they did cast a sunset glow
of gold and color and joy
that made the ruin gleam
like the biblical walls of precious stones.

But when the last shimmer faded
and your dwelling was gone to ashes and earth,
then the stone-work of my hut stood bare
in the merciless light.
Scorched walls, hard and jagged.
No warm light, no flowers, not even moss,

but only hard unhidden stone
strange in the sun and for humankind
no help.

Give me your mildness,
if I'm to carry on down here —
And teach me to smile,
to give, as a parting gift to life
with all its pain,
that smile, that smile you wore
then.

Perhaps he was the mother
and I a child.
His soul was older than mine.
It knew so much more,
it enfolded with tenderness
so endlessly much more.

Or was I his little boy,
his small companion
who thought to help him
while he helped me?

Or was he a guest from the realm of stars,
sent unknown on a mission here below?
And was it that his being
was too much soul
and really *couldn't* breathe the thick air down here?

I don't know. What do I know?
I only know that sometimes
I was a mother that could carry you
and that now I'm only a fumbling child myself.

Are you now carrying me
without my seeing you?
Do I live in the lap of your soul
so that you watch over me?

Was it you who kept me from being run over yesterday?
Is it you who sends me friendly spirits?
You who send the bouquet of red roses

here in a strange city
just tonight, our wedding night? . . .

I walk about your countryside
and the earth is brown like velvet.
The wind is full of heaven
and the light is full of God.

The treetops quiver in space.
Small birds sit together,
swaying like singing flowers
in the blue ocean of the air.

They say you lie in the earth.
But then your shape
is all that clothes the earth:
trees and birds and sunlight —
embroidered on the brown velvet soil . . . .

Ten years after Arnold's death, Mi was returning from a term of lecturing at Pendle Hill in Pennsylvania. It was not easy to come back. No one and nothing needed her. She walked back and forth on the deck of the steamer, meeting older and younger couples who clung to each other in the lowering twilight.

How long it's been since I felt Arnold's nearness, she thought.

She remembered Jung-Stilling — or perhaps it wasn't he — who for nine years was aware of his dead wife's presence and, when at that point the awareness ceased, interpreted it as an indication that her duties had been transferred to other spheres.

Maybe that is how things are, thought Mi. Just then it struck her how right and proper it was that life should be so much harder when one grows old. But it was, indeed, empty, without that exceptional quality of those Arnold-greetings. They had come like a special breath of air, sometimes giving her good advice or a milder tone of voice, often pointing out some beauty or goodness she otherwise would not have noticed. Not to mention, in the most miserable moments, the whispered, "And so we shall simply be glad anyhow" that echoed through the years, causing her first to smile and then really to feel happy.

As she was standing there alone, looking out over the wide expanse of sea, from which the sunset colors had now died away, she heard someone call. She turned. A middle-aged woman got up from her deck chair.

"Pardon me for disturbing you," she said, "but as I was going through the passenger list with some other people, they thought that you were the person named Norlind. Is that right?"

Mi responded affirmatively.

"Are you by any chance related to Arnold Norlind? — I have been very ill. Spiritually I reached the point where I couldn't read devotional books. It was as if I became completely insensitive to them. They did nothing for me. Then someone gave me that thin, little *Veranda* book. I *could* read that, and it helped me to come back to Life again. I know it by heart. But I don't need the words any more. It is as if the very pages give me a feeling of security and light. I have a great need to express my gratitude. Let me now say my thanks to you."

After the conversation, Mi stayed out on the deck. She looked out over the darkening ocean. But something seemed different now.

She felt it the next day, when the ship's radio brought the announcement that Europe was mobilizing and the second world war was about to begin.

Arnold could give gifts to people without their ever having seen him.

READY TO TRAVEL

Meetings

The peculiar fatigue that she could forget when she was occupied with work became all the more persistent. In the autumn of 1934, she had no regular job, but had arranged a heavy schedule of lectures on psychology and mental health at several different locations. She was able to rent a room in the home of a friend in Stockholm.

In this room one night she had a symbolic dream, which she described in a letter to a Danish friend.

> Sharply and clearly I dream that I am on an ocean liner heading out to sea. When it gets far out, I suddenly realize that I'm on the wrong boat and that I am traveling in exactly the opposite direction from where I want to go. I am seized with anguish. I go to see the captain and I appeal to the crewmen to put me ashore any place at all, on some island, for I am going altogether the wrong way. But they shake their heads. It is impossible to go off course. Even greater fear comes over me. I wake up from my own cry out of the depths, "Help me get the right boat!"

A few days later, Mi was lecturing at the University of Stockholm. During the break someone said to her, "You're speaking awfully fast. We can scarcely follow you."

Afterwards two of her friends helped her home to her little room. She had a temperature of 104°. At that point the wave of energy stemming from her determination collapsed. First she had pneumonia (and it was before the days of penicillin), and after that followed a series of other afflictions.

Death *was* approaching. But it took a long time deciding what it wanted to do. She lay in a convalescent home, feeble and sleeplessly staring into space. For weeks she remained in a suspended state, unable to stay in bed, unable to eat. The restlessness of the fever wore her down. Accustomed to being healthy and energetic, she was a difficult patient, constantly wanting to make new efforts and yet without the strength to carry them out.

All the work she had planned for the term had to be cancelled. She was being cared for, yet she had no income. But such concerns did not penetrate her consciousness. Economic support from a foundation and the devoted attention of her sisters and friends seemed beyond her comprehension, as did the many kind letters which she mechanically read through, word by word, yet never clearly understood.

There came a night when the oxygen no longer helped. After consultation, her doctor and friend from their student days at Uppsala, Andrea Andreen, telephoned to summon her closest relatives to her deathbed.

When Mi finally understood what was happening, there surged through her an intense feeling of joy. School was at last going to close for vacation, and she was going to get away from problems and houses and boats and walls of separation.

Could this sudden surge of joy have had some effect? Or was it the powerful injection they gave her to keep her alive until the relatives reached the hospital? Or was it the prayers of her friends?

What finally happened was that the clock of this existence, which had come to a standstill, simply began to move again, ever so slightly, ever so slowly. Death, which would have been so very welcome, just then, turned from her and went away.

To be thrown up on the shore again after having been carried far, far out to sea, was a strange experience. Something — she could not say what — had been taken up into the custody of that great, bright warmth that had enfolded her, something that never seemed to come again, something that really had died forever. A special inwardly attentive way of living was part of what had been lost.

Studying the psychology of religion leads one into peculiar

border regions. One may glimpse the strange blossoming of all-too-human unconscious reactions. St. Birgitta had already recognized that some people who find escape from this world through pious exercises are really trying to avoid unpleasant duties. Envy or a hypocritical nature can produce an exaggerated fervor (Cf. Phil. 1:15). Sentimentality and superficial charm are sometimes mistaken for religious qualities. There are many ways of finding personal outlets under the guise of religion.

Thinking that she would be dealing with only a minor facet of this study, Mi had taken up the phenomena of autosuggestion and megalomania in religiously oriented persons and again came upon the name of James Nayler. He proved to be more than simply an example of this type of aberration, however, for the dying words attributed to him constitute one of the most magnificent religious statements in the English language.

Mi harbored doubts as to whether Nayler had been correctly interpreted in the standard presentations. Working in the unpublished source materials, she found herself compelled to become thoroughly acquainted with this former Cromwellian quartermaster, who was a leading figure in the earliest days of the Quaker movement.

The more thorough study of James Nayler and his strange fate was not in the least likely to divert attention away from the tragic aspects of human religious experience. In the process, she stumbled into a painful conflict between two unusual and deeply religious men whose integrity no one could question.

As in her study of psychology, here, too, she was confronted with the inescapable and discouraging fact of human limitation. But just as convincingly, she was also confronted with that Reality which transcends limitations and whose light can penetrate and redirect even the most limited human being.

She was also more and more captivated by the dynamics of the prehistory and beginning phases of the Quaker movement. For a long time, these studies occupied her completely.

She found certain similarities between the modern situation and that out of which Quakerism arose, contemporaneously with the breakthrough of empiricism in science. The English Civil War, fought by so many "with a Bible in one hand and a sword in the other," despite a victory for democracy, ultimately produced a dictatorship. The outcome brought disillusionment to many who had believed "all the great words." So intensely did they feel the claim of personal truthfulness that they felt obliged to abstain from the naive repetition of those traditional expressions which they could not acknowledge as experienced truth.

In various parts of England, there were groups of earnest seekers, searching for God in a world that had been transformed. Most of them knew the Bible almost by heart. What they thirsted for was to go beyond assertions about the Source to the Source itself, from inessentials to the Essential, or as George Fox put it, "from the Word to the Beginning."

They were not "followers" of anyone, nor had they any theologically trained spokesmen. After the religious breakthrough, they became a comradeship of "finders," men and women who in each new situation listened for "the inward teacher," the Christ within, not only for their individual lives, but also on behalf of the very social order for which they had earlier been willing to sacrifice their lives. Not because of any theoretical principle, but as a result of their historical genesis, their group structure was not patriarchal, but democratic — a fellowship.

They called themselves "publishers of truth" and felt a duty to accept truth from whatever direction it might come. In the midst of terrible persecution, they became champions of religious freedom for others as well, in the certainty that religious truth cannot be coerced but must be experienced. For one after another of these former soldiers, it became a clear obligation to lay aside the weapons of violence, now that they were living in and by "that which takes away the occasion of all wars." There was nothing lukewarm or conditional about their peace testimony. With the primal force of new life, it led old warriors into action and danger for the Kingdom of God.

Certain circumstances made Mi especially receptive toward this movement.

There was that life-determining experience in her youth, an experience wholly without any human mediation. (Assuredly, it was only a point of departure, as she had come to understand all the more clearly.) Then in the years at Birkagården she had so often asked herself how democracy could ever regain its religious roots; in the Quakers she found an answer. From Arnold she had learned to appreciate the positive value of silence. And after the Hague Congress of 1915, the cause of peace, especially peace among the nations, had become ever more compelling.

There was also her view of the contemporary spiritual situation. Right through the ancient and crumbling distinctions, there blows a wind of yearning after *wholeness*. It makes itself felt within the churches and outside them, and not least among those who have discovered the Spirit of Love in the midst of frightful conditions. Such discoverers will surely translate their insight into action more readily than earlier generations could. The yearning has to do with a Reality that is not to be captured in the network of our concepts or even in our symbols, however necessary they may be.

When an epoch has come to an end and died, there is nothing to fall back upon except the Essential itself; no shrouds, only the Living One to whom nothing living is foreign. No "demythologizing" of the New Testament can ever excise the Jesus-image from the inner retina of the Western world. Its beam is radioactive still.

Mi did not know, when she first read *The Nature of the Physical World*, eagerly consuming the final chapter, that its author, Sir Arthur Eddington, was a Quaker. In her diary she wrote:

> After reading Eddington the wonder of life and its all pervading motion became transparently real. As I took my evening walk down to the fisherman's cottage, where some wild ducks swam by the edge of the reeds and a silvery light fell upon the water, I felt that I was touching the mantle of the Almighty. On the way home, as the fading evening glow threw a pale lustre over certain places along the path while others lay in the dark shadows, as the gravel crunched beneath my feet and the wind swept over my face and made a murmuring in the pines — then too the essence of Life opened up.

Then came the memory of a peculiar psychic sensation she experienced some weeks after Arnold's death. It was as if she had within her a warm spot that was constantly refreshed by a ray of heat. If it resembled anything, it was like a shaft of light pouring down through a round skylight onto a point on the floor, leaving the surrounding surface in the shadow of the roof. It was more *real* than so many other sensations communicated by the external senses. The "ray" remained for weeks.

Beneath all these thoughts and impressions there also stirred undiscovered elements from former generations. As she came back to life after her period of illness, Mi clearly perceived that she was only at the beginning of "the journey of the soul." Lying there inactive, she pushed her way farther into another set of circumstances, her ancestry, especially her mother's family, about which she knew most. What her grandmother had meant in her life was certainly as decisive as it was unfathomable.

We are all affected by the past, often without recognizing the source of its indirect influences. When one's world expands, both through insight into the contemporary struggles and miseries, gigantic in their dimensions and with purposes that are hidden from us, and also through new contact with the vein of life coming from generations not far in the past, then one understands better one's smallness in the universe, at the same time that the feeling of community grows and deepens. Knowledge can impart a sense of our common outward fate, but the vital inward kinship of souls is imparted only by love, only by God.

A cry rises up from within us: "Let me meet Thee in all brothers and sisters, being open to what is *theirs* rather than hardening in what is my own!"

And at that there burst through within one a little sprout of new joy.

During Mi's years at Birkagården, Dagny Thorwall's room had provided a place for sharing thoughts about the conflicts that sometimes arose among the students and where friends could be quiet together under the weight of humanity's problems. There were just a few women, colleagues and friends, who used to meet there. For them these gatherings became a source of strength, but they were not part of any larger context or "frame," not even of Birkagården. They occurred quite spontaneously with the initiative coming from Dagny Thorwall, a person whose remarkable influence was well camouflaged by a girlish friendliness and modesty that often allowed people to enjoy a feeling of their own superiority — at first.

In 1927 Karl Heath and several other Quakers had lectured in Sweden. Beginning that autumn, silent worship was held on certain Sundays in the Library at Birkagården. It was Dagny Thorwall and some others at Birkagården, as well as outside it, who met together without being connected with any official Quaker body. After Arnold and Mi moved into Stockholm, they sometimes joined in this silent fellowship.

It has been said that you don't make a Quaker of anyone, you just discover those who are already. The times required one to take a stand by some sort of affiliation. Mi felt that she could unite with the Quakers in complete honesty and perhaps even find among them some task to perform. Toward the end of 1931 Dagny Thorwall and she submitted their application for membership in the English Society of Friends, since there was no Quaker organization in Sweden. The English edition of *James Nayler* appeared just at that time, and, knowing that the book dealt with some of the darker sides of George Fox, Mi considered the possibility that her application might be turned down. Such was not the case, however.

The little group in Stockholm slowly began to grow. The Swedish members decided to arrange a meeting with Archbishop Erling Eidem (of the Swedish Lutheran State Church). When he generously offered to come to them, they met together in the "quiet room" at Birkagården.

The archbishop greeted them warmly and then said the Lord's Prayer in a low voice. In turn he asked each of the ten or so persons present to tell how they had been led to Friends. This was the first time they themselves had heard of each other's personal paths into the fellowship. For some, Dagny Thorwall's study circle had been the decisive influence. Others had come by way of the group in Geneva or some English meeting. Some had been seekers for a long time and had now found their spiritual home in the little group at Birkagården.

"Although all this pains me on behalf of the church," said Erling Eidem, "yet God is still greater than the Church. No one knows what ways He chooses to promote His Kingdom . . . ." The archbishop had a genuine appreciation of silence as a form of worship. He offered a prayer for the group, asking that they might be "fervent in spirit, humble, and willing to serve." He asked them to pray for "your old mother" the Church, and sometimes for himself.

There was solemnity and a gripping stillness in this meeting . . . .

Retreat and Reinvolvement

While on a visit to the old manor house at Högfors Iron Works, Mi learned that a small cottage on the park grounds was for rent. The owner was prepared to modernize it and allow Mi to take her main meal at the manor house. So in the summer of 1946, she moved from Stockholm up to the Bergslagen district. It was an acknowledgment, she thought, that old age had arrived. She would retire into quietness the way old people in India leave the world and go to the mountains.

Here she had smooth lakes, swift-flowing streams, and the wide, silent forests. But there was also a friendly center and the ancient iron works with traditions going back five hundred years. The noise of it eventually became familiar and reassuring, like the sound of rushing water. The flaming torch of the slender smoke-stack rose like a lofty flare against the dark winter skies. One could see the stone-hard ore transformed into streams of red and white fire.

The first months in the country were primarily an opportunity for self-examination. In the last few years, Mi had been given a glimpse of unbelievable suffering. But she saw herself as a person devoid of any solid accomplishment, a kind of jack-of-all-trades of the intellectual profession. In every respect her self-criticism became harsh and sweeping.

She had to get out and walk whenever such feelings beset her. One late autumn day there came this reflection of the landscape:

Grimly the winter twilight comes.
Ice muffles the brook's murmur.
No hoarfrost, no bright crystals,
Heavy clouds, a sunless haze.

The teeth of the dark forest's edge
Bite the bright streak of sky.
All else is leaden grey.
The wind tears at the white birch,
A corpse of summer.

The snow begins.
Its sharp needles fasten in the chilled flesh.
The machinery roars in anguish —

Tonight it's far to God.

The lines poured from her. But as she walked, the versifying halted. It was composed of slag without fire.

With complete immediacy, above the black etching of the landscape upon the eye, it felt as if someone close to her ear were singing, almost in a mocking tone, the words of the old hymn, "He drives away sorrow like the mist." It spoke as to a child with little griefs in a world of desolation. One could not have spoken like that to people who had been in Auschwitz!

She smiled — at her own pretentious claims upon existence, at her wanting to "accomplish something." After all, the last line was wrong about the distance.

There came a fresh wind that turned everything around. At first she didn't want to be faced about, for regrets and gloomy moods have their appeal for someone preoccupied with self.

At last she yielded and smiled — an old retired religion-teacher on her pension! That divine sense of humor. "A sense of humor is the forgiveness of sins," an Uppsala student once said. Now it gave her a shove from behind and the very landscape looked different. Like an obedient child she went back to her little cottage.

One day Mi had a telephone call from the Swedish Mental Health Association, which offered her a position working with doctors in a pioneering project in Västerås. The local health authorities would provide space for counseling sessions twice a week. The work began in the summer of 1947.

She could not tell what permanent value her listening and advice had for her clients. The results were certainly mixed, even though continued contact in some cases seemed encouraging. But she had to admit that the work was of tremendous benefit to herself. To think that she was being useful! Not only did it demand all her energy, but everything that she had ever learned in all her study and training. Occasionally she found a spirit struggling so heroically against accumulated obstacles that she could perceive, through all the banal entanglements, "that of God" in the person, who was usually lacking in any pretense of religious expression.

It took all her strength to empathize, to attempt to grasp the person's whole situation from the inside. At the end of the sessions she would be completely exhausted, physically, mentally and emotionally. It seemed to her that in these cases of private suffering and conflict, she saw a distinct reflection of the misery of the entire contemporary world.

This work experience, this gateway that had been opened for her by complete strangers, was closely associated in her life with that inner event that had once become the determining factor in her course of studies. It aimed at something more profound than the psychological and philosophical questions that had come to concern her. She was led into a way of seeing that she later found very clearly described by Martin Buber. A newly experienced togetherness, a thou-relationship between the creating, suffering, perceiving God and fumbling human beings.

She sought to express it thus:

> There are times when we think life is passing us by. Things happen — or fail to happen — that we regret or approve. But we find that what is happening doesn't really concern us or have anything to say to us. We cannot see ourselves involved in a drama where we have any personal role in shaping the development of the plot or the ultimate outcome.
>
> When we feel that life is "passing us by," this is really an illusion. It is we who have got stuck in the outer shell of material things. We are asleep to the fact that every delight and joy, difficulty or sorrow, every person, creature or thing, every discovery, is a call to us, one that we do in fact always respond to, even when we take no action. World events and occurrences in our everyday life come to *test* us: How do you answer this? Do

you want to, or don't you? Do you know, or not? Do you care whether you see or know or desire or respond?

A reality whispers to us in our joys and sorrows, knocks at the door of our conscience, shakes up our inertia, calls out to us in our misery. The call can sometimes seem to come from a loudspeaker, trying to make us and our whole world finally wake up!

Perhaps we are stubbornly keeping our receivers turned off. At certain calls we become wide awake, but others we refuse to admit into our consciousness. In general, it is much like the situation before radio waves were known. We lived in ignorance of the real existence of such unseen forces.

But there have always been people who have a thou-relationship with all living creatures, such as Francis had. There is "something" about them that can penetrate the barriers we put up around ourselves, a radiance of spirit through their whole beings. It operates not by some theory, but by its *reality*, just as the air fills our lungs long before we understand the function of breathing.

In meeting a *thou* I comprehend something that is not *I*. This discovery takes place most often in the relationship of loving. A very ordinary person can experience a new relationship to existence. It is not he or she or you or I who is remarkable, but simply the new free and open attitude toward someone. This is the element of wonder. *I conceive what is different from myself*. And the whole world takes on a new glow and new possibilities.

To have at some point come upon the *thou*-world is the prerequisite for genuine conversation (which is not merely an occasion for alternating monologues), as well as for the fruitful sharing of silence. There is something in the character of the relationship itself, in the trust and love, that transcends the individuals involved. "For if you believe in a person," said Arne Garborg, "you believe in something that is more than a person."

In this time of great need we encounter, both within and outside the established denominations and formal creeds, fellow human beings who even in the midst of suffering have been profoundly affected by a religious experience which has lifted them up into contact with the great *Thou*, an inescapable *Thou*, who asks new questions and points to new tasks. The message carries meaning not only for our private everyday existence, but even for the larger world with whose fate we are forced to recognize that our own is bound up.

Nor can it be denied that contact can be lost or never established or be changed into remoteness, resistance, indifference or contempt. Just at the point where we have been wounded, bitterness and humiliation can form a hard scar that spreads around the heart like impervious armor. Or it may become a persistent point of hardness and coldness, ultimately a spiritual cancer that nothing seems capable of penetrating. We can also fritter away our thou-potential through a bustling preoccupation or the force of habits that make us more like things that have been folded up than like human beings open and receptive to life. We think we benefit more from what we own or enjoy or perhaps simply would like to have, than from people who oblige us to become bigger, to widen our horizons, to give of ourselves.

A sense of community is one of the deepest needs of the present day, but it can no longer be found in authoritarian regimes. We require community not least as a source of knowledge. But it must be based on a deepened *thou*-sensitivity toward all persons and nations, on that relationship which is the "highest summation of the law" for human life, namely, love. In this very relationship dwells God. "*Das Zwischen*" Buber calls it. Paul quotes Cleanthes: "In him we live and have our being."

Epilogue

A human being is a path. One among the countless paths that started from a family, a people, a culture. One can also have begun from some isolated spot on the outside, and it will ever be noticed in one's manner of walking. There goes someone who asks questions, who stops and asks again, or who rushes blindly ahead, never letting oneself become settled into the shells of certain given concepts — for good or ill.

When "this creature" — to borrow a personal description from the medieval pilgrim Margery Kempe — when this creature looks backward as the end of the journey draws near, there are three childhood memories that come to mind as typical. That they are not in the least original is of no consequence in this connection.

The first — a lack of logical capacity perhaps? The big sisters are pressing the little one: "Whom do you like best, Fej or Nan?" In the face of all their pedagogical explanations and their impatience and anger over the younger child's stupidity, she stubbornly, and at last shrilly, insists, "Fej *and* Nan."

The second: a bridge in one direction can become a barrier in another. To help with weeding the garden, there came a peculiar woman with a little turned-up nose. Because she looked so poor and strange, Mi was attracted to her and hung about the strawberry patch where she was at work. The next morning the old woman pulled out of her pouch a little packet of raisins that she had apparently bought for a few coins in order to please the little girl. (Mi can taste them still — small, hard as stone, dusty and unpleasant!) Mi went inside. But when Mother said that it wasn't good to eat anything that Stina gave her, Mi became fiercely rebellious and disobediently ate them all up, incensed at the terrible injustice that Stina not be allowed to give! Thought proposed a bridge, but reality set up a barrier, this time against Mother. That experience has been repeated.

The third: there is someone — something — *other*, that can irradiate walls of separation, so that it happens as in the words of the old medieval Swedish manuscript: "This thought drives from the heart all anger and pride."

The family were on their way home from the country in a large char-a-banc. An extra person had been invited to ride along into town, and it was crowded. Mi had to lie on a blanket in the bottom of the wagon between the two long seats where the rest were sitting. She was filled with petty irritation at first for being put at the others' feet. Soon, however, she discovered that above her over the wagon was the great gleaming dome of stars, wider and clearer than she had ever seen before, and visible just there from the lowest place. Later, when they wanted her to change and sit up on the seat, all thought of injustice had been completely forgotten and blotted out by the little girl's view of the night sky. Greatness was not just something quantitative. No, it had being, it gave, it transmitted something that was *different*.

Something of this third experience came again more strongly in her youth: "She saw that we all belong indissolubly together in the depths of life."

She saw that her studies — and even those for formal certification had presented no real difficulty — had been basically directed more toward gaining empathy, more toward *understanding* what was different, than toward determining boundaries and making distinctions according to the laws of intellectual labor. Was this simply a lack of ability and nothing more? Or perhaps a repressed ambition on her part? Or was it that such understanding *from within* constituted a vital need in the age to which she belonged?

The work in a pioneering school, the study of new developments in religion and philosophy as an Olaus Petri fellow, the relationships with Anna Lindblad, with Nathan Söderblom and

Friedrich von Hügel — all these stages along the path of "this creature" had shown that the boundaries between different denominations played a far smaller role than the living spirit of unity which she had encountered in people who still "resided" within completely separate communions.

Summers had brought her into direct and sometimes intimate contact with the Swedish peasantry. Myr Peter, Backmor and others had inspired in her a deeper reverence than many more learned persons. There was an immediacy about them, a radiance, without "wrapping paper." One confronted God rather than religion.

Yet in her studies and research, she had clearly perceived the rays of that Reality which *is* truth, and had been thrilled by beauty. On one occasion, though she was quite unmusical, her innermost being had been touched and opened by the tones of the *in nomine Domini* of Mozart's Requiem.

Then of course there was Arnold, who lived ever more completely in the world of radiance and let her experience its power, while she still had lessons left to learn in the borderland — before she got to travel farther in.

FOOTNOTES

Unless otherwise indicated, all the Swedish works cited in the Biographical Introduction were published in Stockholm. Almost all of Emilia Fogelklou's books were published by the Stockholm publishing house of Albert Bonniers Förlag. Only in instances where this was not the case will the publishers of her works be given in the following notes.

1. E. Fogelklou, *Barhuvad*, 1950, p. 13, 18.
2. E. Fogelklou, *Minnesbilder och ärenden*, 1963, p. 44.
3. *Ibid.*, p. 49.
4. *Ibid.*, p. 59.
5. *Ibid.*, p. 51.
6. *Ibid.*, p. 55.
7. *Barhuvad*, p. 57.
8. *Ibid.*, p. 58.
9. *Ibid.*, p. 58f.
10. *Minnesbilder och ärenden*, p. 62.
11. O. Weininger, *Geschlecht und Charakter,* Vienna and Leipzig, 1903, Chapter 12, especially p. 388.
12. E. Fogelklou, *Medan gräset gror*, Vol. 2, 1911, p. 91.
13. *Ibid.*, p. 95.
14. *Ibid.*, p. 99.
15. *Ibid.*, p. 109.
16. *Medan gräset gror,* Vol. 1, p. 174.
17. *Barhuvad,* p. 111.
18. *Protestant och katolik*, 1937, p. 39.
19. *Ibid.*, p. 64.
20. *Ibid.*, p. 77. This quotation from Von Hügel is not given here in its

original English, but in my translation of Emilia Fogelklou's Swedish translation from the English. The original text has not been available to me.

21. *Barhuvad*, p. 173.
22. *Protestant och katolik*, p. 11f.
23. *Barhuvad*, p. 175.
24. *Ibid.*, p. 180.
25. *Ibid.*, p. 202.
26. *Ibid.*, p. 190.
27. *Ibid.*, p. 207.
28. E. Fogelklou, *Förkunnare,* 1915, p. 1f.
29. E. Fogelklou, *Från hövdingen till den törnekrönte,* 1916, p. 50f.
30. *Barhuvad*, p. 242.
31. *Ibid.*, p. 245.
32. *Ibid.*, p. 244.
33. E. Fogelklou, *Arnold*, 1944, p. 59f.
34. In addition to Emilia Fogelklou's book about him, there are articles on Arnold Norlind in most Swedish encyclopedias and biographical dictionaries, such as in *Svenska män och kvinnor*, Vol. 5, 1945, p. 545.
35. E. Fogelklou to Ellen Key, July 26, 1923, in The Royal Library's Letter Collection, Stockholm, HA-L41:55:10.
36. E. Fogelklou, *Kväkaren James Nayler,* 1929; *James Nayler. The Rebel Saint. 1618-1660*, translated by Laila Yapp, London, Benns, 1931.
37. *James Nayler. The Rebel Saint,* p. 232.
38. *The Friend*, London, October 9, 1931. *Supplement*, p. iv.
39. "George Fox and James Nayler," in *The Friend*, London, December 25, 1931, p. 1183f.
40. *Journal of the Friends Historical Society*, London, Vol. 28, 1931, p. 77f.
41. Mab Maynard to Emilia Fogelklou, November 5, 1931, in Emilia Fogelklou Samling, Women's History Archive, University Library, Gothenburg.
42. Hans Larsson, "Emilia Fogelklou," in *Ord och bild*, 1935, p. 407f.
43. S.H. Huveröd, "Hennes tempus är presens," in *Göteborgs Handels- och Sjöfartstidning*, October 16, 1972.
44. Elin Wägner, *Väckarklockan,* Bonniers, 1942.
45. *Arnold,* p. 5.
46. M. Abenius, "Mäktig i tystnad," in *Bonniers litterära magasin*, 1945, p. 45.
47. *Ibid.*
48. *Arnold*, p. 239, 295.
49. E. Fogelklou, *Resfärdig*, 1954, p. 293.
50. *Ibid.*, p. 31.

51. E.H. Linder, *Resor i rum och tid*, Natur och Kultur, 1956, p. 127.
52. E.H. Linder, *op. cit.*, p. 124.
53. S. Stolpe, *Vadstena och andra studier,* Bonniers, 1949, p. 114f.
54. *Arnold*, p. 53, note 1.
55. *Barhuvad*, p. 55.
56. G. Vallquist, "Emilia Fogelklou i minnet," in *Svensk litteraturtidskrift*, 1973, No. 3, p. 38f.
57. E. Fogelklou, *Form och strålning,* 1958, p. 99.
58. R. Fenger, "Emilia Fogelklou på Vejle-seminariet," in E. Fogelklou, *Det aller almindeligste menneske*, Statens Seminarium for Småbørnslaererinder, Vejle, Denmark, 1969, p. 23.
59. K. Westman Berg, "Emilia Fogelklou in memoriam," in *Hertha*, No. 6, 1972, p. 17f.
60. A. Jenhoff, "Minnesbilder från Emilia Fogelklou (Ili) sista tid," in *Vår lösen. Ekumenisk kulturtidskrift,* Sigtuna, 1979, No. 6, p. 315.
61. Erik Sollerman, "Sveriges enda helgon," in *Nerikes Allehanda*, Örebro, September 28, 1972.
62. *Begravningsandakten vid Emilia Fogelklou-Norlinds bortgång*, mimeographed typed transcript, 1972, p. 3-5.

SOURCES FOR THE TRANSLATIONS

The translated material beginning on page 67 of this work has been taken from the standard Swedish editions of three of Emilia Fogelklou's autobiographical books. I have taken certain liberties with the original text, largely in omitting names and references that are familiar only to those American and English readers who are well acquainted with the Swedish cultural history of the last hundred years. The passages selected for translation may be located on the following pages in the Swedish originals: *Bareheaded (Barhuvad*, 1950) pp. 5-39, 44-56, 66-67, 90-91, 95-96, 107-108, and 162-163; (*Arnold*, 1944) pp. 9-20, 24-27, 29-30, 31-61, 185-190, 209-219, 227-254, 259-262, 265-269, 275-280, 281-284, 287-289, 292-296, 299-302, 304-305; *Ready to Travel*, (*Resfärdig*, 1954) pp. 48-50, 55-61, 64-67, 71-75, 227-228, 232-236, 291-293.

A CHRONOLOGICAL BIBLIOGRAPHY OF EMILIA FOGELKLOU'S PRINCIPAL WORKS

(Unless otherwise indicated, the place of publication is Stockholm. Numbers in brackets show pages where the work is mentioned in the text.)

Allvarstunder. Religiosa tanke-och livsbilder; framställda för barn. 1-2, 1903, 1913. (Two volume collection of devotional talks given for school children.)

Om religionsundervisningen. 1904. (Lectures on religious education) [24]

Frans av Assisi, 1907, 1922, 1972. [27, 46.]

Medan gräset gror. En bok om det växande. 1-2. 1911 (*While the Grass Grows. A Book about Growing*) [26.]

Forkunnare. En bok för lekmän om Israels profeter. 1915. *(Proclaimers. A Book for Laymen about the Prophets of Israel)* [38.]

Från hövdingen till den törnekrönte. Några drag ur medeltidens Kristushistoria. 1916 *(From Chieftain to the Man Crowned with Thorns. Some Aspects of the Medieval Image of Christ)* [39.]

Ur fromhetslivets svenskhistoria. 1-2. 1916-1917. (A textbook in the history of religion in Sweden from pre-Christian times to the late middle ages.)

Birgitta. 1919, 1955, 1973. [41f.]

Protestant och katolik. Ett bidrag till fromhetslivets psykologi, Uppsala, 1919. *(Protestant and Catholic. A Contribution to the Psychology of the Devotional Life)* (A second, much enlarged edition was published in 1937) [52.]

Från själens vägar. Religionspsykologiska utkast. 1920. *(From the Ways of the Soul. Sketches in the Psychology of Religion).*

Vila och arbete. Jämte andra föredrag i praktisk psykologi. 1924. *(Leisure and Labor. Lectures on practical psychology.)* [47.]

Befriaren i högtidssägner och bilder. 1925. *(The Liberator.)* (The life of Jesus in scripture, hymns and poetry with illustrations from the paintings of Fra Angelico) [47.]

Människan och hennes arbete i psykologisk-historisk belysning. 1926. *(Man and His Work)* [47.]

Samhällstyper och medborgarideal. 1926. *(Community Types and Citizen Ideals).* [47.]

Skolliv och själsliv. 1927. *(School Life and Spiritual Life)* [47.]

Kväkaren James Nayler. En sällsam gestalt i religionens historia. 1920. *(The Quaker James Nayler. A Singular Figure in the History of Religion* (Published in London in 1931 as *James Nayler, The Rebel Saint, 1616-1680)* [48f.]

Samarbetets psykologi och förvärvslivet. 1929. *(The Psychology of Cooperation and Professional Life).* [47.]

Den allra vanligaste människan. Stadier och vägar. 1931. *(The Most Ordinary Individual. Stages and Ways).* [52.]

Om psykisk hälsovård. Ett försummat samhällsproblem. 1932. *(On Mental Health Care. A Neglected Social Problem).*

Luther and Fox. A Paper Read at the Amsterdam International Conference of Friends. November 1932. London, 1933. [51.]

William Penn. En bok om samvete och stat. 1935. *(William Penn. A Book about Conscience and the State).* Translated by Wolfgang Sonntag and published in Hamburg, 1948 as *William Penn. Ein Buch vom Staat und vom Gewissen,* and in Leipzig, 1963 as *William Penn. Quäker und Staatengründer.)* [51.]

Psykiska faktorer i samband med frågan om krig och fred. 1937. *(Mental Factors in Relation to the Question of War and Peace)*

Bortom Birgitta. Spörsmål och studier. 1941. *(Beyond Birgitta. Queries and Studies)* [55]

Tror vi på det goda? 1942. *(Do We Believe in Goodness?* a sermon*)*

Arnold. 1944, with subsequent editions and reprints. [37, 44, 46, 56, 59f.]

Ljus finns ändå. 1948. *(There is Light Still).* [58.]

Barhuvad. 1950. *(Bareheaded)* [58.]

Helgon och häxor. Essäer. 1952 *(Saints and Witches)* [59.]

Resfärdig. 1954. *(Ready to Travel)* [58.]

Form och Strålning. Åskådningsfragment. 1958. *(Form and Radiance)* [59.]

Brev till vännerna. Urval och inledning av Gunnel Vallquist. 1979. Letters written to Ellen Key, Arnold Norlind, Lydia Wahlstrom, Klara Johansson and others).

INDEX